Table of Contents

Introduction 3

How to Use *Aslan Academy* 7

The *Aslan Academy* 7 Step Plan 11

Overview of *Aslan Academy* Resources 23

Review of Fundamentals 27
    Overview article on Reviewing the Fundamentals 29
    Overview article on Is My Child a Follower of Jesus? 31
    The Need for Covering Prayer 35
    Bible Study on God's Plan for Parents 37
    Issues to Ponder 40

Understanding and Encouraging Heart Change 41
    Overview article on Understanding and Encouraging Heart Change 43
    Bible Study on Understanding and Encouraging Heart Change 47
    Issues to Ponder 50

Developing Character and Faith that Lasts 51
    Overview article on Developing Character and Faith That Lasts 53
    Bible Study on Developing Character and Faith That Lasts 57
    Issues to Ponder 60

Teaching the Bible to Your Children 61
    Overview article on Teaching the Bible to Your Children 63
    Bible Study on Teaching the Bible to Your Children 65
    Issues to Ponder 67

Introducing Spiritual Disciplines to Your Children 69
    Overview article on Introducing Spiritual Disciplines to Your Children 71
    Bible Study on Introducing Spiritual Disciplines to Your Children 75
    Issues to Ponder 79

Helping Children Understand and Explain Their Faith 81
    Overview article on Helping Children Understand and Explain Their Faith 83
    Bible Study on Helping Children Understand and Explain Their Faith 85
    Issues to Ponder 87

Family Read-Alouds 89

Listen and Learn on Their Own 91

Aslan Academy Gatherings 93
    Notes to Leaders 95

Introduction
Intentional Parenting to Disciple Our Children

Why do young people walk away from their faith when they leave home?
Key reasons include their lack of strong faith as a child and their parents not having lived a vibrant faith.

Parents tend to focus, almost by default, on raising kids who will exhibit good behavior, succeed in school and eventually in employment, and become decent citizens. If they accomplish this, most feel, they have parented well.

While these are important outcomes, they are not the most important. What do I desire most for my children? For them to grow in the knowledge and love of their Savior Jesus Christ and articulate, defend, and joyfully live out their faith in whatever calling God has for them. Helping disciple our children on this journey should be a parent's urgent priority.

Deuteronomy 6:5–8 tells us that we are to love the Lord with all our heart, soul, and strength, and commit wholeheartedly to God's commands. We are to repeat these commands again and again to our children when we are home, on the road, when going to bed and getting up.

Proverbs 22:6 notes that we parents are to train our children in the way they should go, and when they are old they will not turn from it. The Bible is clear that parents are chiefly responsible for helping their children become effective disciples. The church can help. Youth groups can help. Godly friends can help. But parents are on the front line, and they need help.

Parents deal with so many seemingly urgent and important things–managing their jobs, helping kids with school, taking them to sports, music, or play practices, church activities, hobbies, vacations … At times, just surviving the daily grind can seem like an impossible goal.

But if we fail to intentionally prepare the hearts of our children to fall in love with the Creator of the universe and find joy in following Him, our work as parents will fall dreadfully short of God's plan for us to lead our children. Likewise, as a church, if we neglect the work of equipping parents to disciple their children, we have forfeited a foundational responsibility.

> *Recent studies from a variety of reputable sources have confirmed that parents, in general, are not properly preparing children to have a solid faith. Here are just a few summary comments:*
>
> Not surprisingly, homes modeling lukewarm faith do not create enduring faith in children. Homes modeling vibrant faith do. So these young adults are leaving something they never had a good grasp of in the first place. This is not a crisis of faith, per se, but of parenting.[1]
>
> The drop-out problem is, at its core, a faith-development problem; to use religious language, it's a disciple-making problem. The church is not adequately preparing the next generation to follow Christ faithfully in a rapidly changing culture.[2]

If parents have a vibrant, strong faith and model that faith for their children, it is much more likely for those children to develop a similar vibrant, strong faith that is maintained throughout their lives.

The culture of a typical middle school, high school, or university seems almost designed to pull children away from their faith. With the plethora of information on the web and through influential messages on TV, movies, music, and other entertainment options, it is more important now than ever for parents to help children fully understand and defend their beliefs. The world is intentional about worldliness. Parents need to be intentional about discipling their children.

Unfortunately, churches are not, and cannot, fulfill the role of discipling our children. Even churches that make this a priority will get a small percentage of a child's time during the year. Without a parent being fully engaged, a child is left to be pulled away in the general cultural tide. To help address this urgent need for discipling our children, the C.S. Lewis Institute has created the *Aslan Academy*, a new program designed to help parents understand the need for—and to provide access to—quality resources to begin and sustain the discipleship process with their children.

There are thousands of available books and other resources—many being helpful, many misguided or even harmful—on the subject of raising godly children. Sorting through the options can be a daunting challenge. We've identified a small number of highly effective resources to help struggling parents begin this exciting journey of discipleship with their children. And each month, through our new *Dawn Treader News*, we will highlight additional resources and provide helpful ideas for the upcoming weeks.

The *Aslan Academy* fills part of our larger vision of developing effective discipleship resources for people at each key stage of life. So much of a person's world view and so many opinions are set before the teenage years, making it crucial for parents to recognize the urgent importance of shaping their child's spiritual growth. As parents, we can't guarantee our children's salvation, but we can prepare their characters and model a vibrant faith that can capture their imaginations and understanding.

For parents who have not been actively discipling their children, don't worry. It is never too late to start.

The *Aslan Academy* program will help you get started no matter where you are in this process.

The program features a biblical overview of the Aslan Academy approach and essential parent preparation, including the following:

- Reviewing the Fundamentals of Faith
- Understanding and Encouraging Heart Change
- Developing Character and Faith that Lasts
- Teaching the Bible to Your Children
- Introducing Spiritual Disciplines to Your Children
- Helping Children Understand and Explain Their Faith
- Family Read-Alouds for Inspiration and Discussion
- Listen and Learn on Their Own
- Monthly updates through the *Dawn Treader News*, with further resources to equip and challenge parents and children

---

To best use the resources of the Aslan Academy, we've produced the Seven Step Plan to guide parents on this journey. Each step is broken down in categories that include: Pray, Read & Study, Apply, and Family Activities. Parents can work through these steps at a pace appropriate for their family.

In addition, we've also launched **Aslan Academy Gatherings**, designed to build a community of parents within a church body who will commit to proactively discipling their children. These regular gatherings are a place to share ideas, exchange resources, pray for families, and encourage one another. Children today are seeking authenticity in their lives and most desire to be challenged. Developing a community of parents who share a real commitment to discipleship can not only dramatically improve their children's lives, but also change the overall culture of the church. These gathering can be led by children's directors on church staffs or by committed parents within churches or in small groups.

C.S. Lewis knew the importance of helping children learn and grow in their faith. Lewis's Narnia series has proven to be one of the most enduring and helpful tools for children to see insights into God's story. These stories are included in the *Aslan Academy* reading recommendations, as well as discussion guides that will help parents reinforce Lewis's core messages.

Lewis's example helps us extend our reach beyond our own children. He spent countless hours responding to letters from children[3], and his care and love for these children—most whom he never even met—can inspire us as we focus on being intentional with our own children and with others in our extended families, our churches, or our neighborhoods. Toward the end of his life he wrote to a child, "If you continue to love Jesus, nothing much can go wrong with you, and I hope you may always do so."[4]

For parents, or grandparents who can play the role, the process of discipling their children should be one of excitement and joy, helping their children come to understand God's nature, His plan for us, and His power to help us live bold, fruitful lives. To walk with a child and help that child learn to love God and then see that love unfold for many years is something we all want to experience. No matter where you are in that process, we believe the *Aslan Academy* can equip and encourage you to be more effective in that journey.

Notes

1 Focus on the Family Findings, "Millennial Faith Participation and Retention," http://www.focusonthefamily.com/about_us/focus-findings/religion-and-ulture/~/media/images/about-us/focus-findings/FF%20-%20Millenial%20Faith%20Retention%20FINAL.ashx, August 2013, 4.
2 David Kinnamen and Aly Hawkins, You Lost Me: Why Young Christians Are Leaving Church and Rethinking Faith (Grand Rapids: Baker Books, 2011), 21.
3 C.S Lewis, Letters to Children, ed. Lyle W. Dorsett and Marjorie Lamp Mead (New York: Simon & Schuster, 1985).
4 C.S. Lewis, The Collected Letters of C.S. Lewis, vol. 3 (San Francisco: HarperSanFrancisco, 2007), 1474.

How to Use This Guidebook
The Purpose of the Aslan Academy Program

The *Aslan Academy* program is designed (1) to address one of the most important needs in our families and churches today—for parents to understand the importance and urgency of beginning and sustaining the process of effectively discipling their children and (2) to provide an easy-to-use approach and a limited list of effective resources to begin that journey.

The Program Approach

Parents face many pressures and complications in raising children today, and there is no shortage of books, articles, programs or plans to help them be effective parents. The problem for many parents is to know where to start.

We've tried to make this a much simpler process, providing parents with a limited number of highly effective books, articles, Bible studies and thoughtful questions to get on a path where discipleship can take place.

We provide parents a recommended Seven Step Plan, where each step builds on the previous step. These steps are to be completed at a pace comfortable for an individual family. Each step integrates a variety of elements including:

 Prayer—how to pray with your child and to build a prayer team to pray for you and your family as you begin the *Aslan Academy* program.

 Read & Study—learning from a combination of short articles, Bible studies, and a limited selection of highly effective books to provide parents a foundational knowledge of the elements necessary for your child's spiritual growth.

 Apply—how to put what you are learning into practice, with suggestions for each step along the way.

 Family Activities—how to help your family develop habits and regular activities that will contribute to spiritual growth.

Key Program Components

The components listed below are incorporated in the Seven Step Plan, sequenced to build on the previous step. Here is a brief description of each component:

Reviewing the Fundamentals
Whether you are a new or long-time believer, it is important to review the fundamentals of the Christian faith before beginning the process of discipling your child.

Understanding and Encouraging Heart Change
Rather than simply seeking behavior modification, it is important to understand that long-term change comes through authentic heart change, driven by the Holy Spirit.

Developing Character and Faith That Lasts
Learning important character traits can assist in deepening faith and will provide a foundation that will help your child persevere through challenges.

Teaching the Bible to Your Children
Children (and parents) need to understand (1) how the Bible is one amazing story of God's love and (2) His plan for redemption. God's Word is essential in helping your children know, love, and understand God's plan in their lives.

Introducing Spiritual Disciplines to Your Children
For centuries believers have developed helpful practices to help them grow in their faith. Parents can use these same disciplines, applied in an age-appropriate manner, to help their child develop and practice a deep faith.

Helping Children Understand and Explain Their Faith
Significant numbers of children leave their faith when challenged in high school, college, or as young adults. Children must be equipped to truly understand what they believe, be prepared to explain and defend their beliefs, and be comfortable sharing that faith with others.

We also offer additional resources to inspire and encourage families as they read together, and resources for children to read or listen to on their own.

Books Needed for the Program

This program requires the reading of a variety of books, usually 1 to 2 books in each section, over the course of the Seven Step Plan, which may take anywhere from six months to a year. The complete resource list is in a separate section, but please note that in many cases parents are asked to read only one of two or three choices; there is no need to purchase all the books to get started. We recommend that parents eventually go back and read all the resources, but it is not necessary up front.

In the on-line version of the *Aslan Academy* you will find links to each of these resources at Amazon.com, which offers parents the choice of new, used, or Kindle versions of the books. Even families on a very tight budget should be able to gain access to these books at a reasonable cost. Most of the books are available on a variety of other websites (e.g., Christian Book Distributors, Cokesbury) and in many bookstores. Parents might also check their local libraries or their church library.

The other resources—Bible studies, short articles, issues to ponder, etc.—are included in this guidebook and are available on the *Aslan Academy* website at www.cslewisinstitute.org/aslanacademy.

Considerations Before Starting

For married couples, the program will have the greatest effect if both parents "buy in" and participate fully in the Seven Step Plan. If only one spouse will be carrying the load, or if you are unmarried, seek a godly adult friend or relative to help you as you seek to disciple your child. Perhaps seek a group of single parents in your church who might simultaneously participate in the *Aslan Academy* program to provide prayer support and a sounding board as you seek to lead your child to know and love our Lord. Whether you are married or single, God loves you and your family and wants you to know Him better and grow in faith.

Examine Your Schedule and Your Child's Schedule

Discipling your child will take time. While the *Aslan Academy* has been designed to work for busy parents, it is important to do some necessary "cleaning out" of schedules before beginning. The program calls for short morning or evening times with your child, for longer discussions at mealtime or other times, and time for occasional activities. In addition, each step in the *Aslan Academy* program asks parents to complete a Bible study, read short articles and one or two books. Last, and perhaps most important, blocking out time to pray for your child and for your efforts to disciple your child is absolutely essential.

Few parents look back and say they wished they had spent less time with their children. Finding time now, even in the midst of busy work, school, and sports activities, is important. If your children's spiritual growth is a priority in your family, that priority has to be reflected in the time allocated to it. Similarly, if you want your children to grow, they must have time in their schedules. Make sure your children are not already overburdened with other activities. Again, if spiritual growth is a priority, it must not be reflected only in your schedule, but also in your children's schedules.

Getting Started

The *Aslan Academy* Seven Step Plan provides a simple, consistent approach that will lead you through the foundational elements of the program and help you develop daily habits with your child. Read over the full list of resources, and choose the resources you will need for the first two steps (carefully noting that often you are given a choice between two resource options). Order the books so you will have them as you complete each step. Be sure to order additional resources in time for later steps. Other than the first step, which should take two to four weeks, the other steps will take four to eight weeks.

Aslan Academy Seven Step Plan

Step 1 — Getting Started: Orientation and Overview

With a focus on foundational prayer–including recruiting a prayer team–plus short articles and Bible studies covering: 1) the fundamentals of the Christian faith, 2) heart change, and 3) the importance of Scripture, this step will get you off to a solid start.

Step 2 — A Good Foundation

By digging into two key books in this section, you will become more grounded in your faith and begin to process the critical issue of heart change. Take the time to write down key lessons learned in this foundational step.

Step 3 — Moving Ahead

A key resource in this step explains how the Bible is one continuous story of God's love for us. You can learn and then explain this to your child. Another short book shares practical guidance on living your faith as a family. More family activities are introduced in this step.

Step 4 — Learning More about How God Made Your Child

In this critical step, the focus is on learning about the unique personality and qualities of your child and beginning the process of character development. Sections of two books are used, plus special outings and family readings begin.

Step 5 — Sticky Faith and Teachable Moments

Learn what makes faith stick and how to take advantage of teachable moments in this step. Add in Scripture memory CD's and suggested meal-time discussions and family outings to keep the momentum going. Don't forget for you and your prayer team to continue praying!

Step 6 — Introducing Spiritual Disciplines

Through one of two books on Spiritual Disciplines, you help your child learn practices to grow their faith. This step also continues the focus on character development and encourages you to assess your child's character while becoming specific in your parenting plans. Readings and outings continue.

Step 7 — Understanding and Explaining Faith

Key resources are introduced in this step to help children begin to deal with tough questions and be prepared to answer them. Family discussions and outings are continued in this step. Parents learn how to recognize signs of real conversion in their child.

Getting Started on the Seven Step Plan

To help parents begin the *Aslan Academy* program and stay focused as they work through the various elements, we offer a suggested approach below. The estimated time to complete each step is listed, but parents should feel free to extend or adjust the times in light of their schedules. We recommend that as parents begin each new step, they write down an anticipated schedule for each listed activity. The Seven Step Plan is designed in a way to help families develop new habits and new intentional approaches to spiritual growth in their children. For each step we offer categories: Pray, Read & Study, Apply, and Family Activities.

We designed these steps with busy families in mind, but discipling children will require a parent's intentional focus. Use the suggested items under each step to build a foundation and then an ongoing pattern of living that will begin to develop your children into disciples of Jesus. Parents often seem willing to make big sacrifices for sports activities, theater, music development, and educational projects and opportunities for their children. While there is value in those activities, doesn't it make sense to place an even higher priority on your child's spiritual development and growth?

For married couples, the program will have the greatest effect if both parents "buy in" and participate fully in the Seven Step Plan. If only one spouse will be carrying the load, or if you are a single parent, try to find a godly adult friend or relative to help you as you seek to disciple your child. Perhaps you can form a group of single parents in your church who might participate in the *Aslan Academy* program and provide prayer support and a sounding board as you seek to lead your child to better know and love our Lord. Whether you are married or single, God loves you and your family and wants you to know Him more clearly and grow in faith.

The following steps will help you begin or, if you are already on this path, help you accelerate that growth.

{ Step One }

Pray

Read & Study

Apply

Family Activities

Getting Started on the Seven Step Plan

(Estimated time to complete: Two to Four Weeks)

Pray

1. Read "The Need for Covering Prayer" in the *Aslan Academy* "Reviewing the Fundamentals." (Page 35)
2. Start praying regularly for your family and your children.
3. Explain to your children that you will be praying for them each day and commit to praying with each child in the morning or evening of each day, in addition to regular mealtimes. Pray out loud for God's guidance and a willing spirit in your child as you begin this program.

Read and Study

4. Read the introduction to the *Aslan Academy* and the section on "How to Use This Guidebook." (Page 7)
5. Read the overview articles that describe the first few sections of the *Aslan Academy* curriculum:
    a. "Introduction: Intentional Parenting to Disciple Our Children" (Page 3)
    b. "Reviewing the Fundamentals" (Page 29)
    c. "Understanding and Encouraging Heart Change" (Page 43)
    d. "Teaching the Bible to Your Children" (Page 63)
6. Work through the Bible Studies for the following sections:
    a. "God's Plan for Parents" (Page 37)
    b. "Understanding and Heart Change" (Page 47)
    c. "Teaching the Bible to Your Children" (Page 65)

Apply

7. Write down key lessons or questions from the articles and Bible studies. Make a list of the steps you are going to take to begin implementing what you've learned.
8. As described in "The Need for Covering Prayer," start recruiting a prayer team. (Page 35)
9. Communicate regularly with your prayer team and share insights gained as you go through this program.

Family Activities

10. Choose an age-appropriate Bible for your child (from the resources under "Teaching the Bible to Your Children") and begin reading from it each day. Or, if the child is old enough, have the child read it on his or her own. Set aside time each day for a brief discussion of the reading.

{ Step Two }

Pray   Read & Study   Apply   Family Activities

A Good Foundation

(Estimated time to complete: Four to Eight Weeks)

 ### Pray

1. Continue praying with each of your children each day, asking God to guide your efforts and work in the hearts of your children.

 ### Read and Study

2. Choose either *Basic Christianity* or *Christianity 101* under "Review of Fundamentals" and read it. Even if you are long-time believer, it is helpful to review the fundamentals to help you as you begin to teach your child.

3. Read either *Parenting Is Heart Work* or *Shepherding a Child's Heart* under "Understanding Heart Change." (Page 41)

 ### Apply

4. Consider "Issues to Ponder" in the "Review of Fundamentals" section of the *Aslan Academy* Guidebook. (Page 40)

5. Consider "Issues to Ponder" in the "Understanding and Encouraging Heart Change" section of the *Aslan Academy* Guidebook. (Page 50)

6. Write down key lessons or questions from either *Basic Christianity* or *Christianity 101*. Make a list of the steps you are going to take to begin implementing what you've learned.

7. Write down key lessons or questions from either *Parenting Is Heart Work* or *Shepherding a Child's Heart*. Make a list of the steps you are going to take to begin implementing what you've learned.

 ### Family Activities

8. Continue daily Bible study or readings from an age-appropriate Bible.

{ Step Three }

 Pray   Read & Study   Apply  Family Activities

Moving Ahead
(Estimated time to complete: Four to Eight Weeks)

Pray
1. Continue praying with each of your children each day, asking God to guide your efforts and work in the hearts of your children.

Read and Study
2. Read *The Big Story—How the Bible Makes Sense Out of Life*. After reading it, set aside time with your child to talk about how the Bible is one continuous story of God's love and His desire to rescue us. Do this over several sessions, perhaps as a story before your child goes to bed.

3. Read *Gospel-Centered Family: Becoming the Parents God Wants You to Be*. Answer the questions under "Questions for Reflection" after each chapter. Write down the key insights you've gained from this book.

Apply
4. Discuss the "Issues to Ponder" from "Teaching the Bible to Your Children" section of The *Aslan Academy* Guidebook. (Page 67)
5. Write down additional issues or thoughts you have from the resources you've completed so far.
6. At unhurried mealtimes, use the "Aslan Moments" (from the *Dawn Treader News*) to guide a discussion each week on key topics. The *Dawn Treader News* can be found on the *Aslan Academy* website at www.cslewisinstitute.org/aslanacademy.
7. Write down a description of your children's faith, their attitudes and their behavior. Discuss your possible parenting shortcomings from the past and begin implementing one or two specific changes based on what you've learned from the resources read so far. Be sure to do a specific plan for each child.

Family Activities
8. Continue daily Bible study or readings from an age-appropriate Bible.
9. Provide some of the "Listen and Learn" resources to your child and allow your child to listen on his or her own or use for car rides and have the whole family listen together. (Page 91) Ask your child about the stories and have him or her describe what he or she is learning.

{ Step Four }

Pray Read & Study Apply Family Activities

Learning More about How God Made Your Child
(Estimated time to complete: Four to Eight Weeks)

Pray
1. Continue praying with each of your children each day, asking God to guide your efforts and work in the hearts of your children.

Read and Study
2. Read the *Aslan Academy* overview article: "Developing Character and Faith That Lasts." (Page 53)
3. Work through the Bible study: "Developing Character and Faith That Will Last." (Page 57)
4. Read Section 1 and 2 of *Raising Kids to Love Jesus*. Write down the unique characteristics of each of your children. Write down your understanding of your child's personality type. Pray for God's wisdom as you learn how to parent each child, based on the child's uniqueness.
5. Read the first five chapters of *Character Matters! Raising Kids with Character That Lasts.* Answer the questions at the end of each chapter. Write down your assessment of each of your children's character under each category listed in the chapters.

Apply
6. Consider the "Issues to Ponder" from the *Aslan Academy* Guidebook section on "Developing Character and Faith That Lasts." (Page 60)
7. From your notes about each child's personality type, write down two or three parenting changes you will make based on this new knowledge, and commit to implementing those changes.
8. From your assessment about your child's character, plan one or two specific steps you will take to begin shaping your child's character in these areas.

Family Activities
9. Continue daily Bible study or readings from an age-appropriate Bible.
10. Plan a special outing with each child to lovingly talk about the positive aspects of what you've observed about that child's personality and character. Praise him or her and celebrate how God has made him or her unique. Reinforce God's love for the child and how He wants to know him or her. Read relevant sections of the Bible to highlight how God wants to shape us to become the person He wants us to be.
11. Begin family readings, starting with *The Lion, the Witch and the Wardrobe*. Use the guide *Aslan in Our World: A Companion to the Lion, the Witch and the Wardrobe* to ask key questions throughout. Look for ways to encourage your children to think and to envision themselves in similar situations.

{ Step Five }

 Pray
 Read & Study
 Apply
 Family Activities

Sticky Faith and Teachable Moments

(Estimated time to complete: Four to Eight Weeks)

 Pray

1. Continue praying with each of your children each day, asking God to guide your efforts and work in the hearts of your children.

 Read and Study

2. Purchase the *Hide 'em in Your Heart* CD (preschool and early elementary) or one of the *Seeds Family Worship* CD's (older elementary and middle school) and play it as you drive around town or allow the child to listen in his or her room. These songs will help you and your child easily memorize key Bible verses.

3. Read *Sticky Faith* to gain insight into what helps children develop and keep a strong faith into adulthood. Complete the discussion questions at the end of each chapter.

4. Read either *The Power of Teachable Moments* or *Faith Begins at Home*.

 Apply

5. From your reading of *Sticky Faith*, write down your assessment of how your parenting approach so far will lead to a "sticky faith." What changes did you see that would be helpful? Commit to implementing at least one change this month.

6. From your reading of either *The Power of Teachable Moments* or *Faith Begins at Home*, write down three specific changes you and your spouse will make to begin creating teachable moments with your children. Commit to do them starting this month.

7. At unhurried mealtimes, begin using the "Aslan Moments" (from the *Dawn Treader News*, the *Aslan Academy* monthly update) to guide a discussion each week on key topics.

 Family Activities

8. Continue daily Bible study or readings from an age-appropriate Bible.

9. Plan a special outing with each child to continue discussing character. Think of an event or activity to illustrate an opportunity for growth.

10. Continue family readings as well as encouraging your child to listen and learn on their own. Once you have finished reading *The Lion, the Witch and the Wardrobe*, continue reading through the *Chronicles of Narnia* with the study guides. Every family is different, and accordingly should adapt the schedule of reading to suit the interests and time availability of family members. Try to read a chapter two or three times per week. If you don't have time to go over all the questions in one sitting, discuss them over the next couple of days, keeping the story fresh in the children's minds and building their excitement to read the next chapter.

 Pray

11. Continue updating your prayer team and seek specific prayers as you learn more about your child's needs.

{ Step Six }

Pray Read & Study Apply Family Activities

Introducing Spiritual Disciplines

(Estimated time to complete: Four to Eight Weeks)

 Pray

1. Continue praying with each of your children each day, asking God to guide your efforts and work in the hearts of your children.

 Read and Study

2. Continue daily Bible study or readings from an age-appropriate Bible.
3. Read the *Aslan Academy* article on "Introducing Spiritual Disciplines to Your Children." (Page 71)
4. Work through the Bible Study "Introducing Spiritual Disciplines to Your Children." (Page 75)
5. Read either *Habits of a Child's Heart: Raising Your Kids with the Spiritual Disciplines* or *Spiritual Disciplines for Children, A Guide to a Deeper Spiritual Life for You and Your Children* under the section on "Spiritual Disciplines."
6. Read chapters 6–10 in *Character Matters! Raising Kids with Character That Lasts.* Answer the questions at the end of each chapter.

 Apply

7. At unhurried mealtimes, pick one of the spiritual disciplines and discuss why it is important and how it might be adopted in your family. As a family, seek to have everyone take an initial step toward following that discipline in an age-appropriate manner. Discuss it regularly as you implement it.
8. From your reading in *Character Matters!* Continue your assessment of each child's character under each category listed in the chapters. Plan one or two specific steps you will take to begin shaping your child's character in these areas.

 Family Activities

9. Continue special outings (perhaps an outing to serve together) with each child or together to continue discussing character and seeking an event or activity to illustrate an opportunity for growth.
10. Continue family readings using the *Aslan Academy* suggested resources as well as encouraging your child to listen and learn on their own. Find time to discuss what they are reading and hearing.

{ Step Seven }

Pray　　　　Read & Study　　　　Apply　　　　Family Activities

Understanding and Explaining Faith

(Estimated time to complete: Four to Eight Weeks)

Pray
1. Continue praying with each of your children each day, asking God to guide your efforts and work in the hearts of your children.

Read and Study
2. Continue daily Bible study or readings from an age-appropriate Bible.
3. Read the *Aslan Academy* article "Helping Children Understand and Explain Their Faith." (Page 83)
4. Work through the Bible Study "Understanding and Explaining Your Faith." (Page 85)
5. Choose the age-appropriate resource under "Understanding and Explaining Their Faith." Begin working through the questions with your child. Take the time to discuss and seek additional resources for help if necessary. Help your child feel comfortable asking tough questions, and, as a parent, commit to finding satisfactory answers through *Aslan Academy* or other resources, your pastor, or children's director at church. Work through the questions at a comfortable pace. This process may take weeks or months.

Apply
6. Consider the "Issues to Ponder" from the *Aslan Academy* Guidebook section on "Helping Children to Understand and Explain Their Faith." (Page 87)
7. Read the article on "Is My Child a Follower of Jesus?" (Page 31) Think about where your child is in terms of his or her understanding of God and salvation. If your child is ready, begin the discussion of what it means to be saved and how your child can place faith in Jesus Christ. If your child has already professed faith, review these key elements and engage your child in the discussion to discern his or her understanding.
8. From the resources under "Understanding and Explaining Your Faith," pick one question to raise at unhurried mealtimes and engage your family in the discussion. Parents should do research before asking the question in order to guide the discussion. Continue this practice from time to time going forward.

Family Activities
9. Continue special outings with each child to continue discussing character and seeking an event or activity to illustrate an opportunity for growth.
10. Continue family readings as well as encouraging your child to listen and learn on his or her own. Find time to discuss what your child is reading and hearing.

Pray
11. Continue updating your prayer team and seek specific prayers as you learn more about your child's needs.

Ongoing Intentionality

If you've completed the suggested agenda for the first seven steps, you will have a good understanding of heart change, building character, the importance of teaching the Bible and spiritual disciplines. You have begun the process of helping your child better understand and explain his or her faith. You will also have begun regular time with your child to read and to talk about spiritual growth. We trust, this time has allowed you and your child to grow closer together as you both seek God leading in your lives.

Now it is time to focus more and more on your child and his or her specific growth needs.

Pray

1. Continue praying with each of your children each day, asking God to guide your efforts and work in the hearts of your children.

Read and Study

2. Continue daily Bible study or readings from an age-appropriate Bible.
3. Over time, go back and read the other *Aslan Academy* resources you may have missed. You will find further insight into each of the main topics.
4. Look for interesting new resources highlighted in the *Dawn Treader News* to further deepen your understanding of discipling your children.
5. If you child is at the stage to begin considering colleges, you and your child should read *How to Stay Christian in College* and discuss the key questions and concepts raised in the book.

Apply

6. Look for evidence of heart change in your child. Find those "teachable moments" to reinforce opportunities to help their heart change.
7. Continue introducing the spiritual disciplines in an age-appropriate manner. Guard against becoming legalistic in your approach. These disciplines are to help your child have a deeper, personal relationship with Jesus, not simply to "earn points" by doing works.
8. Continue working through the tough questions and build confidence in your child's ability to explain his or her faith. Use the apologetics questions from the *Dawn Treader News* to guide these discussions.
9. Update your assessment of your child's personality, heart, character and status of conversion. Continue to be intentional about encouraging positive growth and helping your child address weak areas.
10. If you have a child who is an adolescent or teen, develop a plan to use the resource *Building Character: A Bible Study for Adolescents and Teens,* listed under "Resources in Developing Character and Faith That Lasts." If possible, work with your child and other parents to form a group of children who can go through this nine-week Bible study on their own. Pray about how this might be organized and for God's leading in bringing together the right people. As your child goes through the program, discuss with your child what he or she is learning and how he or she plans to make life changes in response. If it is not possible to organize a group of children to go through this study together, make plans to go through it with your child or together as a family.

Family Activities

11. At unhurried mealtimes, use the "Aslan Moments" (from the *Dawn Treader News*) to guide a discussion each week on key topics.

12. Continue special outings with each child if possible, or as a group, to continue character discussions and provide memorable activities to illustrate learnings and reinforce growth.

13. Continue family readings as well as encouraging your children to listen and learn on their own. Find time to discuss what they are reading and hearing.

 Pray

14. Continue updating your prayer team and seek specific prayers as you learn more about your child's needs.

Conclusion

The process of being an intentional parent never really ends. While the above plan offers one path to help you get started, every family is different. The important thing is to be intentional and begin to develop a specific approach for each child, taking into account the child's uniqueness. Be sure to continue praying and to engage your prayer team, keeping them updated as you go along.

Encourage other families to join you in becoming intentional parents. Plan activities together. Encourage your pastor or church children's director to hold regular **Aslan Academy Gatherings** to help other parents be better disciplers of their children.

Overview of Aslan Academy Resources

The *Aslan Academy* uses a variety of resources to assist in the discipleship process. The articles, Bible Studies and Issues to Ponder are provided. Each section also includes a limited number of books that you'll need to acquire. Note that in many cases we encourage you to select one of two book options for a particular topic. Follow the Seven Step Plan for when to introduce these resources.

Each major section of the Aslan Academy includes the following:

- Overview article describing the particular topic
- Bible study on the topic
- Book(s) on the topic
- Issues to ponder

The Books and other resources we recommend for each section are:

Reviewing the Fundamentals

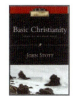 

- *Basic Christianity* – John Stott
- *Christianity 101* – Gilbert Bilezikian and Bill Hybels
- *The Big Story – How the Bible Makes Sense Out of Life* – Justin Buzzard

Understanding Heart Change

 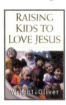 

- *Parenting Is Heart Work* – Dr. Scott Turansky and Joanne Miller
- *Shepherding a Child's Heart* – Tedd Tripp
- *Raising Kids to Love Jesus* – H. Norman Wright and Gary J. Oliver
- *Gospel-Centered Family* – Ed Moll and Tim Chester

Developing Character and Faith that Lasts

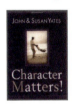  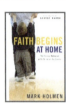 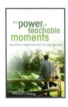 

- *Character Matters! Raising Kids with Character That Lasts* – John Yates and Susan Alexander Yates (Note: this book has also been published under the name Raising Kids With Character That Lasts!
- *Sticky Faith* – Dr. Kara E. Powell and Dr. Chap Clark

- *Faith Begins at Home* – Mark Holmen
- *The Power of Teachable Moments* – Jim Weidmann and Marianne Hering
- *Small Group study for adolescents: Building Character: A Study Guide for Adolescents and Teens* – Developed by Mona Lindeman and Susan Ward (available as a free download at www.cslewisinstitute.org/aslanacademy.)

Teaching the Bible to Your Children

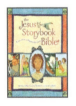  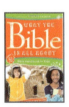

Choose an age-appropriate Bible from the following:
- *Jesus Storybook Bible* – Sally Lloyd-Jones (preschool through early middle school)
- *The Word & Song Bible* – Stephen Elkins (preschool and early elementary)
- *Apologetics Study Bible for Students* – Sean McDowell, editor (for teens, college students, and young adults)
- *What the Bible is All about Bible Handbook for Kids* – Henrietta Mears (through middle school)

Introducing Spiritual Disciplines to Your Children

- *Habits of a Child's Heart: Raising Your Kids with the Spiritual Disciplines* (Experiencing God) – Valerie E. Hess
- *Spiritual Disciplines for Children: A Guide to a Deeper Spiritual Life for You and Your Children* – Vernie Schorr Love

CD's or MP3 Downloads:
- *Hide 'Em in Your Heart* – Steve Green (preschool and early elementary)
- *Seeds Family Worship* (older elementary through middle school)

Helping Children Understand and Explain Their Faith

   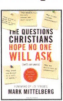  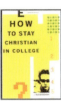

Choose from age-appropriate books from the following:
- *Big Truths for Little Kids* – Susan Hunt and Richie Hunt (preschoolers)
- *The Awesome Book of Bible Answers for Kids* – Josh McDowell and Kevin Johnson (elementary grades)
- *If I Could Ask God Anything: Awesome Bible Answers for Curious Kids* – Kathryn Slattery (middle schoolers)
- *The Questions Christians Hope No One Will Ask* – Mark Mittenberg (for teens)
- *Apologetics Study Bible for Students* – Sean McDowell, editor (for teenagers, college students, and young adults)
- *How to Stay Christian in College* – J. Budziszewski (for high school students anticipating going to college, college students, and parents of high school/college students)

Family Read-Alouds – For Inspiration and Discussion

Choose a variety of books to read to the children from the following:
- *The Chronicles of Narnia* – C.S. Lewis
- *Companion Study Guide: Aslan in Our World: A Companion to the Lion, the Witch, and the Wardrobe* – Cate McDermott
- *Christian Heroes Then and Now* (Series) – Janet and Geoff Benge
- *The Trailblazer Series*

Listen and Learn on Their Own

Choose a variety of the following books for children to listen to on their own:
- *The Chronicles of Narnia Radio Theatre* – from writings of C.S. Lewis
- *G.T. and the Halo Express*
- *Sir Bernard the Good King*
- *Adventures in Odyssey*

Review of Fundamentals

Whether you are a new believer or you've been in church your entire life, we encourage you to review the fundamentals of the Christian faith to prepare you for teaching your children. This section includes articles on reviewing the fundamentals and the critical subject of understanding conversion. It then identifies three basic but thorough guides to give you a strong foundational understanding as you seek to lead your child.

We recommend following the Seven Step Plan as you work through these resources.

Basic Christianity – John Stott

This classic Christian book is considered by *Christianity Today* as one of the most important books of the past hundred years. The author carefully explains the basics of the Christian faith through sections on Jesus Christ (His claims, character, and resurrection), humanity's need (due to sin), Christ's saving work, and humanity's response to God's call. Stott defends the claims of Christianity and then helps the reader live out that faith in daily life.

Christianity 101 – Gilbert Bilezikian and Bill Hybels

The authors provide a simple, but thorough review of the essentials of Christianity, including an overview of all the main doctrines as well as commentary on various interpretations of each. For new believers, this book can provide a solid grounding in the core truths of the Bible. *This book includes discussion questions at the end of each chapter.

The Big Story – How the Bible Makes Sense Out of Life – Justin Buzzard

The author explains the big story of creation, humanity's rebellion, God's plan to rescue us, and the eternal home God has prepared for us. By starting off answering the question of who God is, and who Jesus is, the author lays a solid foundation for understanding the big story. This book is written in a conversational style with lots of stories to highlight each section.

Reviewing the Fundamentals
Article

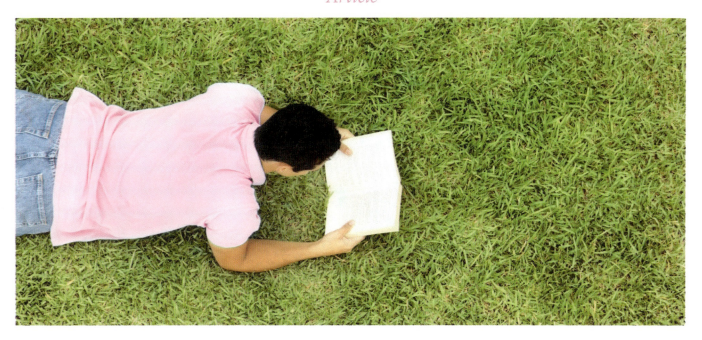

It is quite common for people to assume they have a deep understanding of the Bible. We have learned, however, that even those who have been in church their whole lives, been in small groups, and in other learning environments, often have significant gaps in their understanding of basic biblical concepts.

Surveys of self-identified "born again" believers tell us that there are widely divergent views of salvation, the Trinity, Jesus' incarnation and resurrection, and issues of heaven and hell. Particularly in the West, there is a temptation to pick and choose the doctrines we want to believe and then either set aside or disagree with the more challenging doctrines.

As a parent in charge of discipling your child, you need to understand that it is essential that you take the time to learn biblical truth, and to pass that truth on to your child.

In the *Aslan Academy* Review of Fundamentals, we offer two options for covering the essential doctrines of the church. We encourage each parent to read either *Basic Christianity* by John Stott or *Christianity 101* by Gilbert Bilezikian and Bill Hybels. Either of these short books will provide a clear understanding of the core beliefs of the church. Over time, parents should seek to read both and use them to refer back to address questions that come up.

Second, we offer a short, easy-to-understand book, *The Big Story: How the Bible Makes Sense Out of Life* by Justin Buzzard, which describes how the Bible is one continuous story of God's plan to rescue us from sin. It clearly explains how the Bible is a narrative of God's love playing out over the entire history of the universe and is not simply a collection of disjoined books that describe how we should live.

While written for younger children, we believe *The Jesus Storybook Bible* is a wonderful companion book for adults. The Jesus

Storybook Bible clearly describes how the Bible fits together, with Jesus as the overall focus. Parents will gain much insight as they read along with their children.

Parents should certainly care about their child's salvation, but what this means is often difficult to explain to children. For some parents, once the child "prays the sinner's prayer" they might consider their job done. But in reality it is more complex than that. We offer guidance on how parents should think about conversion and also how to look for clues that true conversion has taken place. And once a child is truly converted, the discipleship work is just beginning.

God wants each of us to grow in spiritual maturity and to offer our bodies (and our lives) as "living sacrifices" (Romans 12:1-2) learning what is good and acceptable to God. And we are called to be filled with the Holy Spirit and to be fruitful, living as effective disciples of Jesus. Conversion is the beginning of this exciting journey, not the end.

Although you may be tempted to "jump right in" with the other steps in the *Aslan Academy* program, please take the time to review the fundamentals and to pray that God will grant you wisdom as you seek to know God's truth and communicate that truth effectively to your children.

Is My Child a Follower of Jesus?
Article

By Joel S. Woodruff, Ed.D.

Christian parents have one ultimate desire for their children—that they place their faith in Jesus Christ as their personal Lord and Savior.

However, what does the conversion of a child look like?

In *The Chronicles of Narnia* book *The Voyage of the Dawn Treader*, C.S. Lewis illustrates what the true conversion of a child looks like. He begins by describing the preconversion life of a boy. He writes,

> *There was a boy called Eustace Clarence Scrubb, and he almost deserved it . . . I can't tell you how his friends spoke to him, for he had none . . . Eustace Clarence liked animals, especially beetles, if they were dead and pinned to a card . . . [He] disliked his cousins . . . But he was quite glad when he heard that Edmund and Lucy were coming to stay. For deep down inside him he liked bossing and bullying . . . he knew that there are dozens of ways to give people a bad time if you are in your own home and they are only visitors.[1]*

This is the picture of a child who doesn't know Jesus. Later in the story, Eustace falls into a dragon's cave with horrifying results. Lewis writes,

> *[Eustace] had turned into a dragon while he was asleep. Sleeping on a dragon's hoard with greedy, dragonish thoughts in his heart, he had become a dragon himself . . . He realized that he was a monster . . . He began to wonder if he himself had been such a nice person as he had always supposed.[2]*

This is the point at which Eustace becomes aware that he is a sinful person, which of course is the first step in the conversion-process. A child must recognize and admit that he or she is a sinner.

Fortunately for Eustace, he soon meets the lion Aslan (the Christ figure in Narnia). Eustace allows Aslan to "un-dragon" him by peeling off his dragon skin. Eustace describes the scene, "The very first tear he made was so deep that I thought it had gone right into my heart,"[3] which of course it had. Eustace's heart has been changed by Aslan, and he is baptized in a pool of water and comes out a changed boy. In other words, the child has repented and confessed his sin, surrendered to Jesus, and the Lord has changed his heart and made him His child.

Lewis then gives us a realistic description of the post-conversion life of a child. He writes of Eustace,

> *It would be nice, and fairly nearly true, to say that "from that time forth Eustace was a different boy." To be strictly accurate, he began to be a different boy. He had relapses. There were still many days when he could be very tiresome. But most of those I shall not notice. The cure had begun.*[4]

In other words, while the child wasn't perfect, there was a marked change in his life now that he had allowed Aslan to "un-dragon" him.

While this illustration can give us an idea about what conversion looks like in a child, how can we know whether or not our child is a Christian?

Fortunately, Jesus gives us some principles to follow in discerning the spiritual state of another person. First, He warns that we must be careful when judging another person; we must hold ourselves to the same standards of holiness with which we critique others (Matt.7:1–5). In other words, whether we're trying to discern the conversion of our child or someone else, we must apply the same basic criteria to ourselves.

Second, Jesus says that it is possible to discern the spiritual vitality of another person by the "fruit" they produce in their lives. Those who are rooted in Jesus will produce good and healthy "fruit." Those who have not experienced the spiritual healing that only Jesus can give will bear "thorns and thistles" (Matt.7:15–20; John 15:4–6). Paul later elaborates on this idea when he says that the follower of Jesus will exhibit the fruit of the Spirit in growing measure: love, joy, peace, patience, kindness, goodness, faithfulness, gentleness, and self-control. In contrast, the nonbeliever will continue to produce the fruit of the sinful nature: hatred, discord, jealousy, sexual immorality, anger, and lying, to name a few examples (Gal. 5:16–25). In other words, our actions are evidence of whether or not our hearts and mind have been transformed by the work of the Holy Spirit. This doesn't mean that Christians will live sinless lives, or that non-Christians will always appear to be bad people. However, there will be a noticeable qualitative difference in the way the Christian lives following true conversion.

Third, Jesus makes it clear that salvation isn't just intellectual assent, merely confessing that Jesus is Lord. He says that on Judgment Day, many will say, "Lord, Lord," and Jesus will say, "I never knew you" (Matt. 7:21–23). Authentic faith in Christ involves a heart that truly believes (Rom. 10:9) and is evidenced by changes in thought, word, and deed. So, while the profession of faith, kneeling by a bedside, or responding to an altar call at church is important, it must be accompanied by a transformation of the heart seen in daily life. What, then, are some reliable signs that someone has experienced true conversion? The great American preacher and theologian of the early eighteenth century, Jonathan Edwards, who preached in some of the revivals of the First Great Awakening, examined this question. In his work The Distinguishing Marks of a Work of the Spirit of God, he found in 1 John 4 that the apostle points out five traits of an authentically converted believer. In modern language, such a person:

> ### Five Marks of True Conversion
>
> 1. Acknowledges and exalts Jesus as Lord and Savior (1 John 4:2–3)
> 2. Recognizes the evil of sin in his or her life, the world, and the devil and seeks to overcome it (1 John 4:4–5)
> 3. Has a growing understanding and love for God's Word (1 John 4:6)
> 4. Seeks for and discerns the truth in all things (1 John 4:6)
> 5. Loves God and others (1 John 4:8)

These five marks of true conversion will be present in the life of every true believer, although the marks may evidence themselves somewhat differently in the life of a child compared to an adult. (Immaturity and stages of development must be taken into account.) So how do these translate into the life of your son or daughter? Here are some questions to consider:

1) Is there a genuine affection and love for Jesus in your child's life, or is your child just parroting your religious language? In other words, is your child in love with Jesus as evidenced by an infectious enthusiasm for the Lord? Does your child enjoy talking about Jesus and demonstrate sincerity in the worship of Jesus as seen in prayers and corporate worship?

2) Is your child truly sorry when he or she does something sinful or harms someone else? Does he or she get upset when bad things happen to others and have a desire to do something about it? Is your child's conscience working in a way that leads to repentance—a change in actions and desire to live like Jesus?

3) Does your child enjoy reading Bible stories, and is he or she growing in the understanding of Scripture? Does your child seem interested in knowing more about God and does he or she ask appropriate questions?

4) Is your child growing in wisdom and is he or she better able to discern good from evil as evidenced by what he or she enjoys doing and choosing? For instance, does a child turn away from media choices that are offensive, recognize and make comments about the bad behavior of adults or peers, stand up for a friend being bullied, and confront or walk away from negative peer pressure?

5) Is your child growing in kindness toward friends and siblings and demonstrating greater obedience toward you as a parent? Is your child respectful toward adults? Does your child play well together with other children—doing kind and thoughtful things for others without being asked?

While the discernment of true conversion isn't an exact science, since only God knows the true state of the human heart, I trust these questions can help you recognize the presence of God's grace in your child. Always keep praying for your child and know that God hears your prayer.

Notes:
1 Lewis. C.S. The Voyage of the Dawn Treader (1952: repr., New York: HarperCollins, 1994), 3–4.
2 Ibid., 91–92.
3 Ibid., 109.
4 Ibid., 112.

The Need for Covering Prayer

As you begin the *Aslan Academy* program, it is important to start praying regularly for your family as a whole and for your children specifically. Find time each morning and each evening to have uninterrupted time with God as you commit to discipling your children.

Consider the following suggestions for prayer:

- Praise God for blessing you with a child or children.
- Ask God to give you wisdom to fulfill your role as a parent.
- Ask God to reveal any hindrances to your faith as you begin the process of discipling your children. Confess any hindrances and ask God for strength to work in you to eliminate those hindrances.
- If you are married, ask God to strengthen your marriage and give both of you a shared, godly vision for discipling your children.
- Ask God to work in the hearts of each of your children, to give them a sense of God's character and His power and His glory.
- Ask God to work in the hearts of your children to give them a spirit of obedience to His commands and to your authority as a parent.
- Ask God to remove the obstacles you may be facing regarding your relationship with your children. Ask for a desire to spend time together and to communicate honestly.
- Praise God for the work He has already done in your life and in the life of your children. Spend time meditating on how God has been involved in your lives.
- Offer to God yourself and your children, to be taught by Him and used by Him for His glory.
- Pray for specific wisdom to better understand the challenges that each child is facing and will face. Pray that God will give you a discerning spirit to guide you day by day in your relationship with your child.
- Pray for perseverance, as the world will seek to distract you from being intentional about discipling your children.
- Pray for protection from Satan, who would love to keep your child from following Jesus.

Recruit a Prayer Team

Ask a group of people you know to join you in praying regularly for you and your family as you begin this journey. Find spiritually mature people in your church, your family, your neighborhood, or among your friends to specifically pray for you and for each child over the coming year. Feel free to share suggestions for prayer possibly in addition to the suggestions above. Send reminders by e-mail and include specific requests as they come up.

Your prayer team is very important to keep you from discouragement and to give you regular encouragement. When you are tired or down, your prayer team can lift you up. Let your child know that others are praying for him or her on a daily basis.

You may find that as you contact people to pray for your children, they may begin a similar process with their children. Invite your prayer team for dinner or regular celebrations during the life of your child. Let your child be encouraged by their prayer warriors, supporting them as they grow into a fully committed disciple of Jesus!

God's Plan for Parents
Bible Study

God calls each of us to a clear purpose: to love the Lord with all our heart, soul, mind and strength. God made this clear to the Israelites in Deuteronomy 6:4–9. Jesus also reiterated this when asked which commandment was the greatest. God, not our children, should be the center of our lives. If our hearts are set on following the Lord, we have taken the first step toward properly raising our children.

As parents, God has given us authority over our children. But we are to exercise that authority with the same love, grace, and discipline that God exercises over us, always recognizing that our children are watching us and are keenly aware of discrepancies between what we teach and what we do. Living out our faith in an authentic, vibrant way is an integral part of teaching our faith to our children.

By participating in the *Aslan Academy*, you are taking the first step toward following God's command. Commit to praying for God's help as you prepare how you will teach and model God's Word and His commands to your children.

1. Read the following verses from the Old Testament (Deuteronomy 6:4–5; Leviticus 19:18) and from the New Testament (Matthew 22:34–40). What two key commands does God make? _____
_____
_____

2. According to the above verses, what should be the center of your life? What might that look like in your daily life? _____

3. If your children look closely at your life, how do you think they would describe your life's primary focus? Ask their opinions. _____
_____

4. Review how you spend your time and your money. See how that matches with how God is calling us to live? _____
_____

5. Write down specific areas of your life that you believe are hindering your ability to love God and love your neighbor. Commit to praying regularly for God's help to refocus your life. _____
_____

6. Read Psalm 127. How does God describe children? How do you see your children as a blessing? _____
_____

7. Read Matthew 18:10–14. How important is it to God that each of these "little ones" come to know Him? How does that change your thinking as a parent? _____
_____

8. Read Deuteronomy 6:4–9. After giving His command to love the Lord with all your heart, soul, and strength, what else does God say to do? _____
_____

9. Read Deuteronomy 5:16 and Ephesians 6:1–3. What does God command children to do? _____
_____

10. Read the next verse in the Ephesians passage (v. 4) and Colossians 3:21. Reflecting on these verses and the passage in Deuteronomy 6:7, what role and responsibility is God giving parents? Why do you think God is giving parents such authority over their children? ___
_____

11. How is God making clear that He expects parents to show grace toward their children? _____
_____

12. God expects children to submit to parents' authority. Jesus is the perfect example with His obedience to the Father (Philippians 2:5–8). Children must be taught to submit to their parents' authority; this involves discipline, done with love. Read the following passages (Proverbs 123:24; Proverbs 23:13; Proverbs 29:15; 2 Timothy 4:1–2; and review Ephesians 6:4 and Colossians 3:21). There are widely divergent views from parenting experts on proper discipline. Based on these verses, how would you describe an appropriate plan and limits for disciplining your children? _____
_____
_____

13. God loves us unconditionally and will never leave us (Romans 5:8; Ephesians 1:4–5; Hebrews 13:5). Read the story of the prodigal (Luke 15:11–32). What does this story tell us about how we are to love our children? _____
_____
_____

14. No matter what you teach your children, they will notice your example. Are you living by what you are teaching your children? If not, list below some of the inconsistencies and repent and commit to seriously addressing these issues. _____
_____
_____

15. In what ways are you setting a godly example for your children? List some of them and thank God for His grace and goodness. Pray that He'll continue to strengthen and empower you to disciple your children. After all, He chose you to be their parents, so He will equip you for what you need. _____
_____
_____

Issues to Ponder for Review of Fundamentals

- Before reading either *Christianity 101* or *Basic Christianity*, would you have considered yourself highly knowledgeable, moderately knowledgeable, or not knowledgeable at all when it comes to understanding the core doctrines of Christianity?
  _____
  _____
  _____

- Where did you get your knowledge of the faith? _____
  _____
  _____

- Does your church do a good job of communicating core doctrines in an effective way? If not, is this something you should discuss with your pastor or another staff member? _____
  _____
  _____

- After reading one of the books in this section, are there significant questions in your mind regarding the fundamental doctrines and teachings of Christianity? What are they?_____
  _____
  _____

- Can you see how personal selfish desires can lead us to believe what we want to believe rather than what the Bible actually teaches? How might this apply in your situation? _____
  _____
  _____

- Do you have a good understanding of how the Bible fits together as one big story? How would you summarize the Bible to your child? _____
  _____
  _____

- What steps will you take in the near future to begin addressing any significant questions you still have about core doctrines?
  _____
  _____
  _____

Understanding and Encouraging Heart Change

As parents, it is easy to seek immediate behavior modification in our children, but miss out on their long-term discipleship. The key is seeking their heart change, not just an improvement in how they act.

While behavior is certainly important, the real work is to have their heart set on God, with a growing desire to please Him. As one author put it, "once this happens, everything else is just mopping up." We recommend that parents follow the suggested Seven Step Plan to fully understand the importance of heart change. Getting this right sets the stage for all growth in the future.

Parenting Is Heart Work – Dr. Scott Turansky and Joanne Miller

This book explains how most parents seek behavior modification in their children, but the important thing is to mold a child's heart for the future. The Bible mentions the word heart more than 750 times, describing it as the center of our being. Once the heart is changed, parents will see not only behavior change; the child's motivations and focus will be changed as well. The authors give strategies to address a variety of challenges parents face.

*This book includes a "Reader's Guide" at the end of the book, which sets forth discussion questions for each chapter.

Shepherding a Child's Heart – Tedd Tripp

The author focuses on foundational areas for biblical parenting, beginning with the issues of the heart, including influences on the child, Godward orientation, authority, examining goals, discipline, and other areas. With a clear emphasis on parents' recognizing the proper goals of shepherding their child, the author provides practical suggestions for accomplishing those goals. The author concludes with advice on shepherding the child through the various stages of childhood.

*This book includes application questions at the end of each chapter.

Raising Kids to Love Jesus – H. Norman Wright and Gary J. Oliver

The emphasis on heart change continues in this book. By cultivating understanding and intimacy with children, parents can plant seeds that will grow, shaping their children in a powerful way. The need to know their child is vastly more important than simply shaping their behavior. The purpose of the book is to help parents cultivate a love for the Lord in their children by effectively modeling and communicating their own relationship with Jesus. Parents shouldn't just provide guidelines but be shepherds. The book has a section that focuses on personality types, highlighting how each child is unique, and how parents should adjust based on their children's personality traits.

Gospel-Centered Family – Ed Moll and Tim Chester

The authors explain how God is rightfully in charge and His teachings are good, laying a foundation for respect for God's authority. By respecting God and a child's parents, a basis is formed for a heart change, which the authors describe as much more important than "succeeding" in life. The authors describe how parents need God's grace and His discipline as they seek to discipline their children. Practical advice on administering appropriate discipline is described. The book offers practical guidance on how parents can develop a loving and durable relationship with their children.

*This book includes questions for reflection at the end of each chapter.

Understanding and Encouraging Heart Change
Article

The Bible talks about God removing our heart of stone and replacing it with a heart of flesh (Ezek. 36:26). In Psalm 51:10, the psalmist writes, "Create in me a pure heart, O God, and renew a steadfast spirit within me" (NIV).

When we become believers in Christ, the Holy Spirit comes to live in us—in our hearts—and through the Holy Spirit we become new creatures. "Therefore, if anyone is in Christ, he is a new creation. The old has passed away; behold, the new has come" (2 Cor. 5:17 ESV). When we become new creatures, our hearts are changed to where our desires are inclined toward the Lord and our desires are less focused on increasingly distant selfish, worldly things.

You have probably seen someone who was transformed so completely that you could scarcely believe he or she was the same person you once knew. I have a friend who, in his youth, joined a terrorist organization, was filled with hate, and sought to harm and even murder those he considered the "enemy." This foul-mouthed, fire-breathing hatemonger is now a mild-mannered, soft-spoken, godly discipler of men. God changed him; in particular, God changed his heart. I'd known him for a year or two when someone told me about his past; I simply could not believe it. There is no way, I thought, that the person I knew could act the way he was described. The Bible is full of examples of heart change. Saul (renamed Paul) is a perfect example alongside my friend. Paul went from being filled with zealous hatred toward Christians to becoming the most successful missionary of all time. Jesus changed Paul's heart, and all of Paul's natural gifts and skills were combined with God's anointing to turn him into one of the most important and successful men who ever lived.

For parents, it is easy to lose heart when we watch our children show such selfishness and often anger at any moment they think something is "not fair" toward them. They can hit, bite, and bully other kids and fight against their parents' authority. Through careful application of discipline, this behavior can often be controlled, but then parents can be surprised at how often it returns in certain circumstances.

There is a difference between compelling a certain behavior through consistent discipline and seeing behavior changed due to a new motivation of the heart. The first may allow a parent accompanying a child to rest easy in public; the second will allow for a lifetime of growth guided by the Holy Spirit.

Our children do need to understand and respect authority—the authority of God and the authority of their parents. But as parents we are called to use our authority not just to require good behavior, but to point our children to the ultimate authority, God. We are called to nurture their love and understanding of God and His plan for their lives. We are called to help them develop a godly character that will help them become more and more like Jesus as they grow up. We are called to surround our children with godly examples, while we prepare them for challenging situations.

In short, we are called as parents to equip our children for the most important decision they will ever make: will they trust Jesus Christ for their salvation and surrender their lives for God to work through them in whatever role God has planned for them.

Many parents think that if they can lead their child to say "the sinner's prayer" their work is done. With children, it is never easy to know how sincere they are or whether they fully understand the implications. Our job is to help our children grow in their understanding and to continue to equip them, encourage them, challenge them, and, in particular, show them by example how to become devoted followers of Jesus.

Every child is different. God has made each child unique, and He has a purpose for each child. As parents, we must be willing to take the time to understand how God has "wired" each child and to help the child develop God-given gifts and become a person of great character. As a child's heart begins to change, parents will see areas that require deeper engagement to encourage continued growth and learning.

In today's society, it is common for parents to expend an enormous amount of energy and resources on developing their child's academic skills, considering the right schools and the best universities. Likewise, many parents of children with athletic ability provide significant opportunities to maximize their potential. Another parent might notice a great musical passion and help that child fully develop that gift.

While these may be worthwhile pursuits, what will be accomplished if our child becomes successful by the world's standards but has a faulty character or is living outside of God's desire? A quick look at the entertainment industry or many of our sports "idols" will demonstrate the heartache and devastation that can be caused by worldly success outside of God's provision.

While it is God who is ultimately responsible for changing the hearts of our children, as parents we can do our part to prepare our children for God's work to be complete. Another way to say it is that God will light the fire, but we can pile up lots of kindling so the fire can burn bright!

When we see a child whose heart has truly been changed, and we see how that child begins to love God and then live out that love by the way he or she treats family, friends, and those in need, it is a beautiful sight. That child becomes teachable in so many ways and will accept our authority as parents because he or she respects God's authority personally.

More important, that child will grow up, perhaps go to college, and begin a career with God as guide, able to discern God's will, and resist the worldly pressures that can lead to destruction.

As you work through the resources in this section on heart change, pray that your child's heart be changed, but also that your heart will continue to change. Pray that God will empower you with wisdom and grace to be a godly example for your child.

Understanding Heart Change
Bible Study

The Bible mentions the heart more than 750 times, primarily to describe our will—our ability and desire to do things, to make and carry out choices. The heart, in this context, essentially describes who we are.

This is not the version of ourselves that we show to the world; it is instead the true self that God sees. "People look at the outward appearance, but the LORD looks at the heart" (1 Samuel 16:7).

The natural state of our hearts is sinful or "deceitful" (Jeremiah 17:9–10), but God wants to change our hearts, and He is willing to do so for those who seek Him. God will change our hearts in a variety of ways, and for those whose hearts are changed, there will be evidence of such a heart change. For some, change will be immediate. Others will take longer. For all of us, having our hearts conformed to God's desire will be a lifelong journey. Work through the following Bible study to get a deeper understanding of how God sees the heart and how He wants to change it.

1. What is the natural state of our hearts? (Jeremiah. 17:9–10; Mark 7:21-22) _____

2. Are we able to keep the darker aspects of our hearts to ourselves, or does God know our true hearts? (1 Samuel 16:7; Psalm 44:21) _____
_____
_____

3. Does God want to leave us with deceitful hearts, or does He desire to change our hearts? (Ezekiel. 36:25–27; Psalm 51:10; Romans 5:5) _____
_____
_____

4. How does God use the Holy Spirit in the process of changing our hearts? (Ezekiel. 11:19; Jeremiah. 24:7; Romans 5:5; Proverbs 3:5–6; Galatians 4:6)_____ _____
_____
_____

5. Read the following verses and write out some of the ways God involves us in the process of heart change.
(Ezekiel 18:30-32; 2 Chronicles 32:25–27) _____
_____
_____

(Psalm 51:10; Psalm 62:8; Psalm 86:11; Psalm 119:36; Psalm 119:145) _____
_____
_____

(Acts 15:9; Romans 10:9–10; Ephesians 3:17; Psalm 51:10) _____
_____
_____

(Mark 12:33; Hebrews 10:16; Psalm 40:8; Psalm 119:2; Psalm 119:10; 1 Corinthians 10:6–10) (Colossians 3:16) _____
_____
_____
_____

6. Review your answers to question 5. See if you found evidence for the following ways that God works in us for heart change. Describe how God has worked in these areas in your life:

Repentance _____
_____
_____

Calling out to God _____
_____
_____

Faith _____
_____
_____

Obedience _____
_____
_____

Gratitude _____
_____
_____

7. In the process of heart change, God works to strengthen and encourage us. Read the following passages and write how you see the Holy Spirit sustaining the process of heart change. (1 Thessalonians 3:13; 2 Thessalonians 2:17; Acts 11:23; Acts 14:17) ___
_____
_____
_____

8. Some of the changes we see as our hearts are being changed might involve the following:
   What we think (Matthew 5:28; Matthew 15:8)
   What we say (Matthew 12:31)
   What we treasure (Matthew 6:21)
   Whether we forgive (Matthew 18:35)
   How we love God and others (Luke 10:27; Matthew 22:37-40; Deuteronomy 6:5; Leviticus 19:18; 1 Peter. 1:22)
   What are some other ways by which evidence would show up in your life? _____
_____
_____
_____

9. Read Galatians 5. When our hearts are changed by the Holy Spirit, and we cooperate with Him in this change, we will see our thoughts and actions shift from a focus on sinful desires to godly desires. Write out the changes you would like to see in your life through this change. Also write out what your prayer is for the changes you would like to see in your children's lives. _____
_____
_____
_____

10. Review question 6. Are there any of these key approaches missing in your life? If so, write them down here and pray regularly for God's help to continue the process of changing your heart. _____
_____
_____
_____

Issues to Ponder for Heart Change

- Can you recall a time in your life when you believe that your heart was changed by God? _____
  _____
  _____

- If so, how would you describe that change to your child? What specific things changed in your life? _____
  _____
  _____

- Do you have a friend or member in your church who has been clearly transformed by God? Have you ever asked that person to share his or her story with your family? If not, will you? _____
  _____
  _____

- Do you consider your child a follower of Jesus? Consider your child's conversion story and discuss what changes you may or may not have seen in your child since that event. _____
  _____
  _____

- What areas are you investing heavily (time, money, energy) into your child's development? Sports, education, other activities? How would you prioritize these areas in order of importance in your child's life? _____
  _____
  _____

- How would you describe your family's investment in the spiritual development of your children? _____
  _____
  _____
  _____

Developing Character and Faith That Lasts

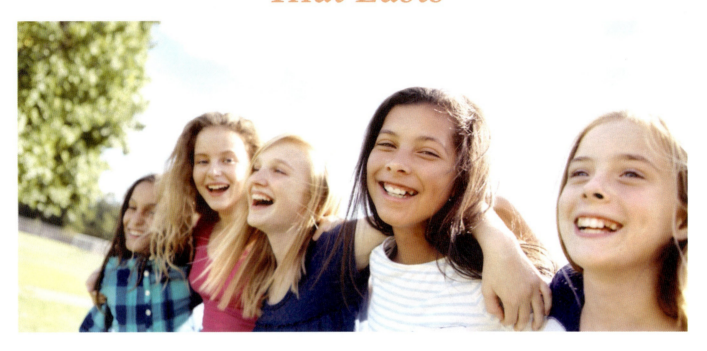

Research shows that a significant percentage of youth leaves the church during high school and college years. Parents need to understand the pressures and challenges facing these youth and provide comfortable opportunities to deepen their children's faith in a way that will allow them to persevere during the challenging years of early adulthood. The following resources describe the problems and offer practical solutions to help. Follow the suggested Seven Step Plan as you work through these resources and apply them with your children.

Character Matters! Raising Kids with Character That Lasts – John Yates and Susan Alexander Yates

This book helps families learn eight essential character traits that matter: integrity, faith, a teachable spirit, a servant's heart, self-discipline, joy, compassion, and courage. Parents and children together can learn how to develop these essential character traits through reading and discussion, then implement them through normal, daily events. Includes focus questions and a leader's guide for use in group study as well. (This book has also been published under the title *Raising Kids with Character That Lasts.*)
*This book includes discussion questions at the end of each chapter.

Building Character: A Study Guide for Adolescents and Teens – Developed by Mona Lindeman and Susan Ward

This nine-week Study Guide is designed for preteens and teenagers to explore what it means to be a person of character. The study is designed to be led by preteens or teens in a group on their own, but would work equally well with an adult leading or as a family. During the study, participants find out what God has to say about certain character traits and think about how they might build those traits into their own character. The study is based on the book *Character Matters! Raising Kids with Character That Lasts,* by John Yates and Susan Alexander Yates, and explores the following character qualities: integrity, self-discipline, a servant's heart, faith, a teachable spirit, compassion, courage, and joy. The studies use a variety of methods to teach the traits, ranging from children creating artwork to participating in role plays.

Sticky Faith – Dr. Kara E. Powell and Dr. Chap Clark

Why are children raised in the church walking away from their faith? The most important finding in the authors' research is that children are shaped by how their parents model and live out their faith. This book explores the findings in their years of research, then focuses on practical application. The authors help parents understand what it means for their children to truly trust Jesus and not simply adopt a "gospel of sin management." The practical advice focuses on three areas: "teach kids that obedience is our response to trusting God, frame all family discussions and activities as opportunities to know and trust Christ, and respond with grace when your child misbehaves." The book covers shepherding children from elementary years through college.

*This book includes discussion questions at the end of each chapter

Faith Begins at Home – Mark Holmen

This book shows how to become a vibrant, healthy family through the concept of a "makeover" in family relationships. The focus on heart change is essential in order to avoid simple moralism. The author shares practical ideas for activities to do as a family and suggested discussion questions for parents to engage children at key moments in their day.

*This book includes a section at the end of each chapter with questions for small-group discussion.

or

The Power of Teachable Moments – Jim Weidmann and Marianne Hering

This Focus on the Family book teaches parents how to use teachable moments to connect their children's life to godly truth. Teachable moments require three ingredients: (1) a good relationship between parent and child; (2) an event that can serve as a catalyst to conversation; and (3) a biblical truth with which to connect. The key requirement is time—time for parents to spend with their child to allow such moments to happen. The book gives practical advice on how to make such time available and to make the most of the opportunities.

Developing Character and Faith That Lasts
Article

In our Western society, the daily pressures mount to help our children excel in school, in athletics, in service projects . . . to "build a résumé" that one day will help them get into the right schools, help them land that first job, and get them started on a productive adult life.

With the rise of social media comes increased opportunities for our children (and ourselves) to self-promote and be compared to others. The pressures in these "social spaces" are usually toward presenting only the most appealing version of our "self" to the world.

If we, as parents, are not careful, we become accomplices in setting our children on a path toward an inordinate preoccupation with "the self" and worldly accomplishment. But do we want our children's "identity" to be built on how they perform or on their identity as a child of God? If we start our children on the wrong path, the world is happy to push them in that direction, reinforcing the belief that accomplishment and promotion is what really matters.

But is this really how we can best prepare our children for their adult years?

Wouldn't you rather have a child whose identify is in Christ, and who grows into an adult that exhibits the "fruit of the spirit" (Gal. 5:22–23)? When people interact with your child and see love, joy, peace, patience, kindness, goodness, faithfulness, gentleness, and self-control, wouldn't you feel that your child is ready to find his or her way in the world?

The Holy Spirit brings the fruit into our lives, but as parents we can help our children's hearts be attuned to the Spirit as we focus on character formation. As parents, we need to help our children develop the inner qualities that will serve as a foundation as they mature into honorable and godly adults.

If our children develop an honorable and godly character, they will be prepared to face adversity with perseverance; selfishness or rudeness with kindness. When they are attacked in some way, they will be able to restrain their reaction with self-control. At school, in the neighborhood, in group activities, they will become an instrument of God's kingdom at work.

Shaping our children's character is not a check-the-box process. It is an ongoing effort to truly understand the child, discover areas of great potential and concern, and then provide guidance through activities that help mold that character into what God desires.

Each child is different; as parents we need to help each child develop God-given gifts and skills, while helping the child turn away from areas that run counter to God's desires.

In this section of the Aslan Academy, you will learn about developing character in the following areas:

- Integrity
- A teachable spirit
- Self-discipline
- Compassion
- A servant's heart
- Courage
- Faith
- Joy

Helping to shape your child's character is a critical part of your child's continued spiritual growth. This section of the *Aslan Academy* builds on the excellent work by John and Susan Yates, as described in their book *Character Matters! Raising Kids with Character That Lasts.*

A significant percentage of children raised in church-going homes drift away from faith as they go from high school through the college years. Simply sharing biblical knowledge and "dragging them to church" won't necessarily instill in them a strong yearning to know God and to follow Him as they become independent young adults. But if children, being led by their parents, have the chance to fully understand the important elements of a godly character and what it means to live an honorable and godly life, they will be more prepared to enter the pressure-cooker world and be able to maintain their faith in Jesus Christ.

A recent study was conducted on Christian students transitioning to college, seeking to understand the most important influences on shaping their faith[1]. From choices of friends inside their youth group, friends outside of their youth group, youth leaders, parents, and adults in their congregation, the students chose parents as the number-one influence. In fact, as pointed out in the *Aslan Academy* resource Sticky Faith, one study concluded that the most important influence in shaping the spiritual life of a child is the spiritual life modeled and taught by his or her parents.[2] So character formation is not just for the children. As you as a parent go through these resources and seek to build a godly character in your children, examine yourself and seek God's guidance your own ongoing character development.

This section builds on the earlier discussion of "heart change." As a child's heart begins to change, the child will become more interested in becoming the person God wants him or her to be. Without heart change, children may learn to "follow the rules" or have decency and manners, but they will miss the big picture of God developing them into the individuals He wants them to be. As parents, focusing on character, rather than selfish promotion and worldly accomplishment, will give children the best opportunity to fulfill God's plan for them. Then, in whatever setting, they will be effective and godly models, maybe even leaders, exhibiting a godly character for others.

Notes:
1 Dr. Kara E. Powell and Dr. Chap Clark, Sticky Faith: Everyday Ideas to Build Lasting Faith in Your Kids (Grand Rapids: Zondervan, 2011), 19–23.
2 Christian Smith with Melinda Lundquist Denton, Soul Searching: The Religious and Spiritual Lives of American Teenagers (New York: Oxford University Press, 2005), 56.

Developing Character and Faith That Lasts
Bible Study

There is a big difference between helping our children be happy and helping them have a godly character that will sustain them through the good and bad periods of life. The foundational elements of character development—integrity, a teachable spirit, self-discipline, compassion, a servant's heart, courage, faith, and joy—take hard work and intentionality on the part of parents. If we neglect character development, much of our other work as parents will easily fall apart as our child leaves our home. As with heart change, the Holy Spirit does the work of change, but as parents we can prepare our children for when the Holy Spirit does His work.

Character development is integrally connected with heart change. Consider character development as the "living out" of heart change in every aspect of one's life. With a godly character, based on biblical teaching, we can weather the inevitable storms and flourish no matter our circumstances. As parents, one of the best gifts we can give our children is to properly prepare them for when they are on their own. Teaching and training them in character development is perhaps our most important job. As you address the questions below, see how God prepares people in each area and how God wants to prepare you and your child's character.

1. Integrity. Read Colossians 3:1–7. If we are raised with Christ, what are we to set our hearts on? _____
_____
_____

2. Read verse 5. Why do you think God wants us to "put to death" our earthly nature? _____

3. A Teachable Spirit. Read Psalm 25:4–15. In verses 8–10, why should we trust God's teaching? _____

4 How do you think forgiveness allows us to be guided by God's teaching? _____

5. Self-Discipline. Read Luke 9:23 and 2 Timothy 1:7. How does the concept of denying yourself lead to a stronger character? Why is Jesus such a strong example for us? _____

6. In 2 Timothy, Paul writes about God's help for us in self-discipline. Why is it essential to have the Holy Spirit give us power to discipline ourselves? _____

7. Compassion. Read Isaiah 58:6–11. Why do you think God describes those with compassion as a "well watered garden, like a spring whose waters never fail" (v. 11)? How does being compassionate not only help others but change ourselves? _____

8. Read Psalm 103:6–14. In your own words, describe God's compassion toward us based on these verses. _____

9. A Servant's Heart. Read Philippians 2:3–4 and John 13:1–17. Why does God call us to value others more than ourselves? _____

10. If Jesus can model service as He did in the passage in John, what types of actions could we model in our life that would demonstrate humility and love for others? _____

11. Courage. Read Deuteronomy 31:6. Why should we not be afraid? _____

12. Read Ephesians 2:10. If God is with you, and we are created in Christ Jesus to do the work God has already prepared for us, what should our attitude be as we go about this work? How can we expect God to help us carry out His plan for us? _____
_____
_____

13. Faith. Read Psalm 111. Write five reasons why we should be able to trust God and have faith in Him. _____
_____
_____

14. Read Ephesians 1:17–21. Describe the power that God describes He will give us as we put our faith and hope in Him. ____
_____
_____

15. Joy. Read John 15:1–13. How do you think the "pruning" process can lead to joy? Describe an experience in your life where this has happened to you. _____
_____
_____

16. Read Psalm 97. Contemplate God's awesome power as described in this psalm. How can God's power and glory help us have joy in our everyday lives? _____
_____
_____

*The elements covered in this Bible study are based on those identified in the book Character Matters! Raising Kids with Character That Lasts, by John Yates and Susan Alexander Yates, one of the resources in the *Aslan Academy* program.

Issues to Ponder for Developing Character and Faith That Lasts

- Think of the key people in your life who have influenced your character the most. Have you ever told your children about these people and how they made an impact on you? If not, why not do so? _____
_____
_____

- Think of your children's closest friends. How would you describe the character of those friends? _____
_____
_____

- Would you describe your child as mostly influencing his or her friends or being influenced by them? Are you taking any steps to help your child be a better influence?
_____
_____
_____

- How has your parenting approach focused on character building so far? Are there other areas that are taking time away from opportunities to build character? If so, what are they? _____
_____
_____

- Based on your estimate of your child's faith, is it likely or unlikely that their faith will stand up to the pressures of high school or college? Think of situations or experiences that might give you insight into the depth of your child's faith. _____
_____
_____
_____

- How would you describe your child's youth group at church? Is the group helping to equip children with a deep faith, or does it seem to be more focused on entertaining them? Have you ever discussed this with your church's youth director? _____
_____
_____
_____

Teaching the Bible to Your Children

Many children learn about Adam and Eve, Noah, Jonah, David and Goliath, Daniel, Jesus, and, sadly, that's about it. While these stories are important, most children are never taught how the Bible is one amazing story of God's love and His plan of redemption, and the stories are connected through this narrative. Giving children a good overview allows them to put these stories into perspective, particularly when it comes to understanding Jesus and why it was necessary for Him to come and save us. The resources below will provide that solid overview and illuminate the entire biblical story in an engaging style.

Jesus Storybook Bible – Sally Lloyd-Jones (preschool through early middle school)
This is our favorite children's Bible. The author explains in a loving and compelling way how "every page whispers Jesus' name." It gives an amazing overview of Scripture, connecting the dots between the Old and New Testaments, between prophecies and their fulfillment in Christ. Beautifully illustrated and written in an engaging, almost poetic, prose, this book will give every child a deep understanding of God's love, His plan to rescue us, and His desire to have a relationship with us. What's more, adults will be drawn in by the beautiful writing as they share it with their children.

The Word & Song Bible – Stephen Elkins (preschool and early elementary)
This Bible presents Scripture through recorded songs and sounds that children under ten will love learning as they follow along with the illustrated book. It has a chapter for every book of the Bible, including a song on an accompanying CD. It is great for children to use during a quiet time each day or while riding in a car. By covering each book of the Bible, this book goes well beyond the typical children's Bible, which tends to focus on only a few stories.

What the Bible is All about Bible Handbook for Kids – Henrietta Mears (through middle school)
This book is adapted for children from the classic, best-selling work by Henrietta Mears. There are separate chapters for each book of the Bible, laid out in easy-to-read form and illustrated for children. For each book of the Bible, this handbook explains who wrote it, the focus of the book, an outline, the main characters, and how the book connects to Jesus. Maps, diagrams, and

cartoon-style dialogue make it an easy, fun read for children and a helpful companion to their Bible. The handbook also has a useful dictionary of key terms in an appendix. This book can be particularly helpful when read along with the Bible, whether in family reading time or when the child is reading alone. Understanding how the Bible fits together can be difficult for children, but this book explains it in a clear, compelling fashion.

Apologetics Study Bible for Students – Sean McDowell, editor (for teens, college students, and young adults)

Studying the Bible can be difficult for anyone, particularly young people. The *Apologetics Study Bible for Students* provides helpful introductions to each book, extensive commentaries on key biblical passages and thoughtful answers to the tough questions young people are asking today. Additional features include "challenges and tactics" for addressing challenging questions, archaeological facts to buttress the historicity of the Bible, and inspiring personal stories of individuals defending and living out their faith. A wide range of effective and credible writers have been gathered to write the extensive features accompanying the Scripture.

Teaching the Bible to Your Children
Article

"Study the Scriptures diligently," Christ said in John 5:39, "these are the very scriptures that testify about me." (NIV)

Every historical narrative, every prophecy, every law, every theological argument contained in the Bible is a link in the chain of God's development of His plan of salvation for humanity. The Bible is the whole story—God's story and message for humanity.

Someone who was asked to give only one reason for why he or she believes the Bible is the whole Truth might reply, "Because it is the only book that accurately describes reality and how to deal with it." In philosophy classes in universities, philosophies are taught, often quite logically and neatly, but they can be pushed into self-contradiction. Not one of these innumerable systems for "living wisely" is in fact liveable. The Bible, and Christianity, is. Even non-Christians cannot help admitting that the Golden Rule is infallibly honorable, that forgiveness somehow leads to the most perfect exercise of justice, and that the central gospel truth of Christ's sacrifice has changed the world as nothing else ever has or could. The complexity of human life—the tangle of sins and emotions and desires and relationships—is only fully explained and dealt with by the Bible. There is nothing more important to teach our children as we prepare them to deal with life in this world.

And the Bible itself is clear that it is the responsibility of parents to teach their children the Scriptures. "Impress them on your children. Talk about them when you sit at home and when you walk along the road, when you lie down and when you get up" (Deut. 6:7 NIV).

This Biblical mandate also describes the most effective method for fulfilling the duty it commands parents to undertake. The best way to teach children about the Bible is to talk about it. Bring up connections between the passages you have read and the issues the world or your family is currently facing. Answer the questions the children ask and ask them some yourself. You might be surprised by the ready grasp children have of spiritual truths. You might find that they figure out with astonishing understanding the meaning of a passage of Scripture that has puzzled you and many other adults.

It can also be helpful to set aside some time for memorizing Bible verses with your children. Committing scriptural passages to memory is the most certain way to ensure access to their guidance in every crucial experience in life. Often the moments that require us to make the most serious decisions occur at times when we may not have a Bible ready at hand. So choosing Scriptures for our children to commit to memory is a meaningful and practical task. Requiring our children to put effort into memorizing Scripture as they would into training for a favorite sport, or learning a leading part in a play, or studying for the SAT, reinforces for them just how important the Bible is and how much a deep and intellectually instructed knowledge of God's Word is necessary in their life.

But precisely because biblical knowledge is necessary for life—true, genuine, eternal life—we must impress on our children the importance of living it out. Children will not make a connection with past occurrences and moral principles unless they see the import they have for their daily life. When reading the Bible with our children, we must show them not only how all the biblical stories connect to form one cohesive narrative of God's salvation, but also how this salvation has changed our lives. Children tend to imitate what their parents do rather than merely act on what they have said. To grow in godly grace and provide a genuine example to their children of what a life lived according to the Bible should look like, parents must spend time in the Word themselves, over and above family devotions with their children.

As your children grow in the Word, they will be transformed by it. It is a wonderful thing to be raised in the Word from the time one is very young; one's habits of thinking and desiring are then shaped in accordance with biblical truths rather than cultural influences. Only the Bible can truly make us realize the way God intended we should live, being "transformed by the renewing of our minds" (see Rom. 12:2). And this transformation leads to the greatest joy one can possibly have: living a real, godly, fulfilled life. We all want something beyond the false, insufficient realities offered to us in the mundane concerns and aims of worldly societies and functions. And the Bible shows us the way to enjoy life to the fullest, life as God really created it to be. If we desire the best for our children, we can do nothing better for them than to raise them with a full appreciation and ever-increasing understanding of the Bible.

Teaching the Bible to Your Children
Bible Study

The Bible is God's story that He wants us to know. Understanding how the Bible fits together into one story of God's plan is important for us individually, but particularly important as we teach the Scripture to our children. Parts of the Bible can seem confusing to children reading on their own, but we can help them understand why Scripture is important, where God's Word comes from, and how it can be used to help us live our lives.

1. Read 2 Timothy 3:16–17. Where does Scripture come from? _____
_____
_____

2. Why is it important for you personally to keep in mind that Scriptures are inspired by God? _____
_____
_____

3. Describe how the Scriptures can be useful in the following areas:

a. Teaching _____
_____

b. Rebuking _____
_____

c. Correcting _____
_____

d. Training _____
_____

4. How do these uses of Scripture "equip us for every good work?" _____
_____
_____

5. As parents, how are we to put into practice what we are told to do in Ephesians 6:1–4 and Deuteronomy 6:4–9? Describe some interesting and innovative ways you can teach the Bible to your children. _____
_____
_____

6. Read 2 Timothy 3:14–15, the verses preceding those read in question 1. Paul affirms that Timothy was taught the Scriptures from childhood. How might such a lifelong exposure to Scriptures be an asset to one's Christian life? _____
_____
_____

7. Read Luke 24:13–35. How does Jesus describe what Moses and the Prophets were writing about? _____
_____
_____

8. Since Jesus claims that Moses and the Prophets were writing about Himself, how does this change your understanding of the Old Testament Scriptures? _____
_____
_____

9. In one paragraph, describe the overall story of the Bible. _____
_____
_____
_____

10. Based on the selections in the *Aslan Academy*, which Bible is age appropriate for your child? Will you commit to spending time reading and discussing the Bible with your child each day? _____
_____
_____

Issues to Ponder for Teaching the Bible to Your Children

- Has reading the Bible been much of a priority in your life? If so, when did that begin and why did you become more interested in reading it? If not, will you make it a priority now? _____
_____
_____

- Has there been someone in your life who really read or taught you the Bible? What about that experience made it interesting?
_____
_____
_____

- After you read *The Big Story*, how did your understanding of the Bible change? _____
_____
_____

- Consider how your family is involved in reading the Bible. How would your child respond if asked whether or not reading the Bible is a priority in the family? _____
_____
_____

- Consider ways you might make it fun and interesting to read the Bible and discuss various Bible stories as a family. _____
_____
_____
_____

- Have you ever used an example from the Bible to illustrate a dilemma or decision that your family has been involved in? How might you do more of this going forward? _____
_____
_____
_____

Introducing Spiritual Disciplines to Your Children

The Bible teaches us to learn Scripture, meditate on it, pray, fast, and always be renewing our minds.

As discussed by numerous church fathers and mothers over the centuries, spiritual disciplines can help us grow in our understanding of our faith and be better equipped to obey God's teachings. The following resources are designed to help equip parents and children to make these disciplines part of daily life. We recommend following the Seven Step Plan to help you understand spiritual disciplines and develop these disciplines in your children.

Habits of a Child's Heart: Raising Your Kids with the Spiritual Disciplines (*Experiencing God*) – **Valerie E. Hess**
This book is inspired by Richard Foster's classic, *Celebration of Discipline,* but is designed for parents to use in teaching their children. The author provides helpful hints on how to teach the disciplines to children in three age groups: early childhood (4–7), middle childhood (8–11), and adolescence (12–15). The book describes each of twelve disciplines, how to practice them, and how to teach them using age-appropriate ideas and exercises. Disciplines addressed are meditation, prayer, fasting, study, simplicity, solitude, submission, service, confession, worship, guidance, and celebration.

or

Spiritual Disciplines for Children: A Guide to a Deeper Spiritual Life for You and Your Children – **Vernie Schorr Love**
Also inspired by Richard Foster's classic, *Celebration of Discipline,* this book is designed for adults to shepherd their children to an intimate relationship with Jesus Christ. By encouraging the "formation of spirit, character and mind towards Christ," a

child will begin the walk on the path toward spiritual maturity. The author helps parents and children understand the tools of spiritual disciplines and their practical uses, with suggested activities for each discipline. As with the above book, the disciplines addressed are meditation, prayer, fasting, study, simplicity, solitude, submission, service, confession, worship, guidance, and celebration.

Hide 'Em in Your Heart – Steve Green (preschool and early elementary)

To help your children memorize Bible verses, these CDs are excellent. Children sing along with musical artist Steve Green, who first introduces each verse, then sings the verses set to catchy music. Excellent for car rides or listening at home.

Seeds Family Worship CDs (older elementary through middle school)

Seeds Family Worship CDs are another great way to help your children learn and memorize Bible verses. The CDs set Bible verses to catchy music which children (and parents) can sing along to. Titles include Seeds of Courage, Seeds of Faith, Seeds of Character, and many more.

Introducing Spiritual Disciplines to Your Children

Article

What are spiritual disciplines? It's not a phrase we commonly hear today, even at church.

Spiritual disciplines are very straightforward, practical steps toward developing a Christian character and a deeper relationship with God.

Most of us have heard of several of them—prayer, worship, service, fasting, celebration—although we may not have seen how they are all connected.

Why do we need these spiritual disciplines? Once we have been saved through Christ, why do we need to do things to discipline our spiritual nature? Well, even though we are redeemed, we are also fallen. Our corrupted human natures constantly fight against our renewed spiritual nature, so we must make it strong, putting on "the whole armor of God" (Eph. 6:13).

Furthermore, as C.S. Lewis frequently pointed out, humans are material as well as spiritual beings. What we believe must be expressed in action, or we will soon lose those beliefs. Maria von Trapp, whose family became famous through the musical *The Sound of Music*, put it this way in her autobiography: "as long as we live here on earth, we simply are not pure spirits, but we also have . . . a very human heart, and that heart needs outward signs of its inward affections."[1]

And it is actually more effective to teach kids about Jesus through spiritual disciplines than it is to try to get them to "feel" converted. We learn truths as children through traditions and habitual practices that we come to identify with what is important in life. Learning and practicing spiritual disciplines will help children to ground their faith more firmly and live it out intelligently and with purpose.

It is essential to teach children spiritual disciplines before they go out into the world and find themselves in situations where their faith will be tested. They cannot be expected to exercise righteous judgment in the world unless they have previously learned and assimilated the virtues that will enable them to make the right decisions when faced with an attack on their faith.

Below is a brief description of twelve spiritual disciplines and brief guidance for incorporating their practice into your children's lives.

Meditation on the Word of God is an essential foundation for forming godly character in your children. When you read the Bible with your children, spend time discussing what you have read. The article on "Teaching the Bible to Children" in the *Aslan Academy* Guide adds more detail on this cornerstone of our faith.

Prayer is probably the first spiritual discipline most Christian parents teach their kids. Even so, it is important to make prayer a meaningful part of life for our children. One of the best ways to help your children understand the importance of prayer is to ask them to pray for you, about issues that concern your family or the world. This will help children to understand that prayer is one of the most wonderful ways through which God enables us to take part in caring for His Creation; that when we pray, we are actually participating in addressing the concerns we are bringing to God to solve.

Fasting is a spiritual discipline less often undertaken today. However, fasting is an important way to prepare ourselves to depend on God rather than material objects for security, which will then enable us to resist more seductive temptations. Fasting from meat, in the early church, would have been a direct stand against the wasteful extravagance of Roman banqueting. Today, perhaps it is better to fast from the junk or "comfort foods" we turn to instead of God, or from the information devices that take up our time—time that might otherwise be dedicated to Him.

Study is different from meditation in that it is more active. Meditating on the Word begins to instill a godly character and a natural bent toward and desire for making godly decisions. But it is also necessary to learn how to apply these Christian principles in the situations of daily life. The more we study the Bible, and how the church has applied its teachings throughout the centuries, the better we and our children are equipped to carry them out today.

Simplicity is all about giving and humility. C.S. Lewis pointed out that the desire for more "luxuries [than] any man can really enjoy"[2] is rooted in pride and enmity, exhibiting the desire to be better than others. Demanding more than we need is a sin deeply rooted in our fallen nature. We are called to set our children the example of generosity, teaching them "it is more blessed to give than to receive" (Acts 20:35 NIV).

Solitude is time alone with God—an addition to prayer. Encourage your children to take the time each day to silently notice and appreciate God's goodness—outside, looking at His creation, is often the best way. Learning to "be still and know" (Ps. 46:10), in awe of God's greatness, is the beginning of reverence and obedience to His will.

Submission is this obedience to God's will. But God has created the parent-child relationship to teach obedience to Him through learning obedience to parents. Our modern society pushes the idea of self-realization. But this rebellious attempt to "make our own decisions," ironically leads to slavery to social fads and sinful impulses. Only God knows what is truly best for us, and obedience to Him and His chosen ministers for our care is the only way to be truly free. Don't feel guilty about imposing Christian rules of behavior on your children; if you don't teach them God's ways, the world will force its ways on them.

Service is putting into practice the two greatest commandments: love God and love your neighbor. Give your children opportunities to serve others. Operation Christmas Child is a wonderful way to start. Teach them that doing God's work and helping others comes first, before taking care of their own personal goals—and that even their talents are God's gifts to be used for serving others, not our own glory. When you ask your children to help out, remind them that this is an opportunity to be a "good and faithful servant" (Matt. 25:21), the highest commendation that can be given us by God.

Confession of our sins is not a one-time conversion event. It is connected with our remembrance of Christ's sacrifice for us; the more often we confess our sins, the more closely we are drawn into the renewal of our lives through His death and resurrection. It is best to have our children ask for forgiveness from God, as well as the people they have hurt, every time they misbehave, and talk to them afterward about the joy of being forgiven.

Worship is honoring God for His greatness. It is easiest to start with gratitude, perhaps by making a list of all you and your children have to be thankful for. Praise and reverence, reminders of His sovereignty, are connected to our joyful confidence of intimate communion with Him. God is King as well as Father, and our worship should contain awe as well as trust. *The Chronicles of Narnia*, with their depiction of Aslan, teach this very well.

Guidance is dependence on God, rather than ourselves, to make the right decisions. It is active faith; when we—and our children—follow God's guidance in His Word, we demonstrate our trust in Him.

Celebration! This last spiritual discipline underscores all the others. Being a follower of Jesus is fun; it is a life of joy. Even times of hardship can become times of celebration, if we seek to understand how God works through those difficult in order to shape us. And every celebratory achievement in our lives, even those not directly connected with worship, can and should be to us opportunities for thanking God for His blessing.

As your children learn that these spiritual disciplines were intended by God for us to rejoice in and grow closer to Him, they will begin to astonish you with their joy and zeal.

Notes:
1 Maria Augusta Trapp, The Story of the Trapp Family Singers (1949; repr. New York: Image/Doubleday, 1990), 73.
2 C.S. Lewis, Mere Christianity (1952: repr. London: HarperCollins, 2002), 123.

Introducing Spiritual Disciplines to Your Children
Bible Study

Having quiet time alone with God is a difficult exercise for many people. For others, it is the time of day when they joyfully come before the creator of the universe and have fellowship with Him. Jesus needed time alone with the Father. We are commanded to do the same.

In today's world, distractions come at us at a feverish pace. Unless we are intentional about time with God, time in the Scripture, worship, celebration and other disciplines, the world will gladly fill our time with urgent, but less-important tasks. As parents, we should not only refocus on these disciplines ourselves, but also begin cultivating these habits in our children. When these habits start early, they will prepare children to continue them as they grow older. That said, these disciplines are outlined to grow your child's relationship with Jesus, not simply to be done legalistically. As parents in an age-appropriate manner support their child's heart change and encourage a godly character, these disciplines can be a part of that development.

The following study questions are designed to give you a small taste of why spiritual disciplines are important. Parents should follow the Seven Step Plan to learn more about applying these disciplines.

1. Meditation. Read 2 Timothy 2:7. Why do you think it is important to "think" or meditate over all that God says? _____

2. In this verse, God says He will "give you understanding in all things." How does "thinking" also include listening to God's voice? _____

3. Prayer. Read Matthew 6:5–13 and Romans 8:26. From these passages, how would you describe the importance of prayer? _____

4. How is the Holy Spirit involved in our prayers? _____

5. Study. Read Romans 12:2. What is the purpose of studying and learning the will of God? _____

6. How can the exercise of our mind be used by God in transforming us? _____

7. Fasting. Why do you think depriving oneself of food, a pleasurable activity, or a habit would cause you to focus more on God? _____

8. Read Acts 13:2–3 and Acts 14:23. Luke describes prayer, worship, and fasting. How would you describe how these three things work together? _____

9. Simplicity. Read Luke 12:15 and Matthew 6:19-21,24. How would avoiding greed and not storing up treasures on earth help someone lead a simpler lifestyle? _____

10. What are some of the pitfalls one would avoid by living a simpler and more modest lifestyle? What are some advantages to this type of lifestyle? _____
_____
_____

11. Solitude. Read Psalm 62:5–8 and Psalm 46:10–11. The author talks about "finding rest" and says to "be still" before God. How can being quiet before God lead to greater understanding of His goodness, His faithfulness, and His trustworthiness? ___
_____
_____
_____

12. Submission. Read James 4:1–10 and Ephesians 5:21–33. Why do you think God wants us to have a humble spirit? Why is He calling us to submit to Him and to each other? _____
_____
_____
_____

13. If you are married, how are you modeling God's command to love and to submit to and respect one another? How would you describe your children's willingness to submit—to God or to their parents? _____
_____
_____
_____

14. Service. Read 1 Peter 4:8–10 and James 2:14–26. How does God use grace to prepare us for service? How would you describe how grace and service can work together to help us grow in maturity? _____
_____
_____
_____

15. Confession. Read 1 John 1:8–9. If we claim we have no sin, what does the author say we are doing and what state would we be in?_____
_____
_____

16. What is the connection between confession and forgiveness?
_____
_____
_____

17. Worship. Read Revelation 4:6–11. Name some additional reasons—why you see God as being worthy of worship. _____
_____
_____
_____

18. Guidance. Read Psalm 139:23–24 and John 16:13. In Psalm 139, David is asking for God to search him and lead him. Why? In John 16:13, through what power does God promise to guide you? _____
_____
_____

19. Celebrate. Read Exodus 23:14–17 and Luke 15:32. Why do you think God was calling His people to celebrate three times each year? Why was the father celebrating the return of his lost son? _____
_____
_____

20. Read Psalm 35:27 and John 10:10. How can celebrating lead us to have joy in God and to have joy in the life God has given us?
_____
_____
_____

Issues to Ponder for Introducing Spiritual Disciplines

- Surveys show that a very small percentage of believers practice any spiritual disciplines other than prayer and reading the Bible. How has your family discussed the other disciplines in the past? _____
_____
_____

- What concerns do you have about beginning to practice the other disciplines as described in either *Habits of a Child's Heart* or *Spiritual Disciplines for Children*? _____
_____
_____

- Are there small steps that your family could take soon to begin implementing one or more new disciplines in an age-appropriate manner? _____
_____
_____

- How would you describe each practice to your child? How can you make it clear that these are not legalistic rules or "works" that are required for salvation? _____
_____
_____

- How would you describe the benefits of these practices to your children? _____
_____
_____
_____

Helping Children Understand and Explain Their Faith

Studies show that a significant percentage of children walk away from their faith when challenged in high school, college, or in some other arena. The vast majority of these children never had a solid understanding of their faith or knew how to explain what they believe. They may have never felt comfortable asking difficult questions, or perhaps they couldn't handle the peer pressure. It is our job as parents to help ground our children's faith, provide a comfortable environment to handle doubts and questions, and help children make their faith real and substantial, able to stand up to the challenges ahead. Follow the Seven Step Plan to use the following resources, broken down by age group.

Big Truths for Little Kids – Susan Hunt and Richie Hunt (for preschoolers)
The authors use catechism to pose questions and provide answers to teach the essentials of biblical knowledge. The overall goal of the book, in the words of the authors, is to (1) Teach children that they are created for God's glory, (2) Show the practical implications of this life purpose, and (3) Repeatedly emphasize to children their need for God's grace to glorify Him. The book has stories that go along with each section of the catechism. Children are expected to regularly memorize sections of the catechism with the long-term goal of memorizing them all. They will then be a guide for that child throughout life. The catechism covers the nature and character of God, the fall, the promise to Abraham, the Ten Commandments, the Lord's Prayer, and so forth.

The Awesome Book of Bible Answers for Kids – Josh McDowell and Kevin Johnson (for elementary grades)
Ideal for children through sixth grade, this book provides simple but clear answers to the questions most elementary schoolchildren have about the Bible. Broken down into helpful sections, the authors tackle questions about God, sin, forgiveness, God's love, prayer, Jesus, the Holy Spirit, the Devil, the Bible, different religions, right and wrong, the future, the church, death, and heaven. The authors also include a short conversation guide for parents as they discuss each of these questions.

If I Could Ask God Anything: Awesome Bible Answers for Curious Kids – Kathryn Slattery (for middle schoolers)

This book is organized into sections on God, Jesus, the Holy Spirit, the Bible, Christianity, prayer, the church, Christian holidays, being a Christian, and "big questions." Focusing mostly on the core truths of the Bible, this guide provides an excellent foundation to help middle-schoolers understand truth and to grow in their faith.

The Questions Christians Hope No One Will Ask – Mark Mittenberg (for teens)

This book by Mark Mittenberg (co-author with Lee Strobel of the Case for Christ series) takes on the major obstacles to belief, helping the reader properly prepare to discuss these issues. Key topics include the nature and existence of God, evolution, can the Bible be trusted, was Jesus just a man or God, evil and suffering, abortion, homosexuality, hypocritical Christians, and heaven and hell. The author provides solid answers and clear context for the answers, done in a loving and winsome manner to prepare teens to effectively engage their friends and others on difficult issues.

Apologetics Study Bible for Students – Sean McDowell, editor (for teenagers, college students, and young adults)

Studying the Bible can be difficult for anyone, particularly young people. The Apologetics Study Bible for Students provides helpful introductions to each book, extensive commentaries on key biblical passages, and thoughtful answers to the tough questions young people are asking today. Additional features include "challenges and tactics" for addressing challenging questions, archaeological facts to buttress the historicity of the Bible, and inspiring personal stories of individuals defending and living out their faith. A wide range of effective and credible writers have been gathered to write the extensive features accompanying the Scripture.

How to Stay Christian in College – J. Budziszewski (for high school students anticipating going to college, college students, and parents of high school/college students)

The author, a professor of government and philosophy at the University of Texas, understands from experience that from the moment students set foot on the contemporary college campus, their Christian convictions and discipline are assaulted. The goal of the book is to prepare, equip, and encourage Christian students planning to go to college, and ones already there, to meet the spiritual challenges of college, and to help parents understand what their children are going through so they can offer more effective spiritual support. The book guides readers through the maze of campus realities, discusses the foundations of the Christian faith, and directly addresses the different world views and myths that students encounter at college.

Helping Children Understand and Explain Their Faith
Article

Many believers, especially those who are young, can relate to this experience of a recent college graduate:

> *I clearly remember the day, during my first semester in college, when I first fully realized how important it is to have learned how to defend your faith as a young person. I was sitting in my Latin class, right before my professor arrived, listening with unbelieving ears to the easy, light-hearted manner in which my fellow classmates—intelligent, cultured young people, most of whom I liked very much—were discussing, and actually laughing about, issues whose sinfulness I had up to that moment sincerely believed no one could underestimate. All at once I realized how different the culture of the world is from the core beliefs of the Christian faith, and how much intelligent effort is necessary in order to explain to others, not only what is truth (John 18:38), but why the truth matters.*

Why does it matter? Being able to defend and explain the Truth of our faith to others is an essential part of our mission to share the gospel with all nations and all cultures. When a person's perspective on life is completely contrary to the Word of God, that person will not understand why he or she needs the gospel, until it is explained to them and his or her own perspective is challenged.

First Peter 3:15 reads: "Always be prepared to give an answer to everyone who asks you to give the reason for the hope that you have. But do this with gentleness and respect" (NIV). This is the chief reason why we, as followers of Jesus, must be able, and train our children to be able, to give a defense for our faith: God has commanded us to do so, but we are to do it with gentleness and respect.

Apologetics, this "giving an answer for your faith," is a part of mission that has been greatly neglected in recent generations. It is easy to see why. Many people are afraid they will not be "smart" enough to undertake properly this great responsibility, forgetting that God's grace is as sufficient for this as for any other task. But in recent years things have become even more challenging. Up until recently, Western culture has been predominantly Christian in its norms and customs. Few felt it necessary to explain why Christianity was the best route to follow. Even the most unchristian members of society knew they had to behave in accordance with at least a superficially Christian moral and philosophical code, even if no one could explain what the reasons were that such moral and religious standards were demanded.

But this has changed. Step into any university across the United States—and indeed Canada and Europe as well—and you will find young people, not unreasonably, refusing to associate themselves with a faith that they do not understand and do not see many people around them purposefully living out. New religions and atheistic philosophies have replaced our nominally Christian culture with a religiously pluralistic culture, and young people see no reason why the faith of their parents and grandparents should be considered more valuable or true than any other.

And this is not happening only on college campuses. In high school and even before, kids are bombarded with questions about and challenges to their faith, whether from friends or through topics raised in our media culture. At such a young age, they cannot be expected to respond from experience; believing adults may well be able to argue against non-Christian world views because they tried them previously and found them failures. Children lack the moral experiences of adults.

However, when it comes to the fundamental questions of reality, children often have a deeper insight than adults. With fewer life complications and responsibilities than adults, young people are often more focused on "big picture" issues, trying to figure out what life is all about without the distractions of career or long-term relationships. They are the ones who are asking the most tricky questions about faith, the ones who most deeply demand an answer.

But how do we teach children how to explain their faith and defend their beliefs when challenged? First of all, it is necessary to recognize that the questions children ask are important; they need an intelligent response. If you as a parent don't have a good answer, say so, but then follow up and do some research. Take time to discuss matters of faith with them. If you demonstrate that you think following Jesus is worth exploring, they will follow your lead in an astonishing way. Children tend to give their all, with fewer culturally induced inhibitions or embarrassment than adults have, to any effort they think is significant in their lives. If they feel that way about their faith, they will likely have a great influence on their friends and classmates and continue to have an influence in God's kingdom work.

Understanding and Explaining Your Faith
Bible Study

As followers of Jesus, we are commanded to share our faith with others. However, most churchgoers are reluctant to do so. Part of that reluctance is that most believers are not prepared—they have not studied or planned—to be able to give an answer for why they believe.

The Bible not only commands us to share our faith, but it also gives us wonderful guidance on how to do so. Through the Bible study below and the other *Aslan Academy* resources in this section, you and your children can be prepared to share faith in a winsome, joy-filled way. Follow the Seven Step Plan for using these resources in an effective way. With the cultural backdrop of today's world, it is more important than ever for believers to give an answer for their hope.

1. Read 1 Peter 3:15. What do you think it means to "be prepared to give an answer" for the hope you have? _____
_____
_____

2. In what way are we to give our answer? _____

3. Read John 3:16–19. When describing your faith in Jesus, how can this passage be an encouragement to nonbelievers? In verse 19, how does this explain how some people are not interested in hearing about Jesus? _____
_____
_____

4. Read Matthew 28:18–20. What does Jesus mean by "making disciples"? Does this seem broader to you than simply seeking "conversions"? _____
_____
_____

5. Read Colossians 3:12–14. What should our attitude and actions be toward those with whom we are discussing our faith?
_____
_____
_____

6. In verse 14, what is the most important thing we must have as we live out our faith? _____
_____
_____

7. Think of the people with whom you regularly come into contact. What are some cultural barriers or difficulties you could expect if you have a conversation about faith? _____
_____
_____

8. List some possible ways you can prepare to overcome these difficulties. Are there questions you could ask that would lead you into an opportunity for a deeper discussion? _____
_____
_____

9. Prepare a three-minute and a five-minute explanation of how you came to a saving faith in Jesus. Commit to be prepared to share that testimony when the opportunity arises. A simple outline to consider is "I was once [fill in the blank], but Jesus changed me by [explain]." _____
_____
_____

10. Using the *Aslan Academy* resources, will you commit to practicing situations with your children so they can be comfortable sharing their faith with their friends? _____
_____
_____

Issues to Ponder for Helping Children Understand and Explain Their Faith

- If someone asked you to explain what you believe about God, how comfortable and clear could you be in answering them? _____
  _____
  _____

- Have you ever asked your child to describe what they believe and why? _____
  _____
  _____
  _____

- How would your child react if a teacher or another student ridiculed his or her faith? Would your child be prepared to give a clear response? _____
  _____
  _____
  _____

- Has there been someone in your family or a close friend who has stepped away from his or her faith because of something bad happening? What are the misconceptions about faith that would cause someone to blame God when trials come? _____
  _____
  _____
  _____

- In conjunction with one of the resources recommended above, ask your child how he or she would answer questions that others might ask about his or her faith. _____
  _____
  _____
  _____

Family Read-Alouds
For Inspiration and Discussion

Finding time to read aloud together as a family will provide great teachable moments and tremendous memories for your family. While there are countless options available, we offer a few series that should make this family time exciting and memorable for children from preschool through middle school. Follow the recommendation in the Seven Step Plan as you introduce these read-alouds to your family.

The Chronicles of Narnia – C.S Lewis

The world of Narnia comes alive through seven stories from C.S. Lewis. Lewis wondered how God's story might play out in another world, and he set out to create that world of Narnia with powerful and memorable characters, chief among them the mighty Aslan who represents Jesus. Good, evil, betrayal, rescue, tremendous friendships, and exciting adventures all await the readers of this series.

Aslan in Our World: A Companion to the Lion, the Witch and the Wardrobe– Cate McDermott

This is the first book in the *Aslan in Our World* Guide Series, which is designed to lead readers into discovering the connections between the principles of Narnian adventure and the truths of Christian theology. The book includes thought-provoking questions, Scripture references, and discussion topics that study groups, families, or individuals may use. Additional titles in this series will be forthcoming.

Christian Heroes Then and Now – Janet and Geoff Benge

Through this series of stories, written in an adventure style, the family will be inspired by the powerful lives of people such as Eric Liddell, Corrie ten Boom, David Livingstone, C.S. Lewis, George Müller, Jim Elliot, and many others. By learning about the struggles and triumphs, children will learn how God has worked so powerfully in others' lives. Published by YWAM (Youth with a Mission), these stories provide excellent opportunities for family discussions.

The Trailblazer Series

Children learn about real-life Christian heroes through fictional lives of children whose stories become intertwined with people such as Martin Luther, William Tyndale, Frederick Douglass, Jonathan Edwards, and more. Written in an engaging style, children will learn about some of the heroes of the faith, and parents can use this material for deeper discussion.

Listen and Learn on Their Own
(for preschool through middle school)

The Chronicles of Narnia Radio Theatre – from writings of C.S. Lewis
Produced by Focus on the Family, these classic stories from C.S. Lewis are beautifully dramatized by talented actors and compelling music and sound effects. Your child will be enthralled by these recordings, which run more than twenty-two hours (on 19 CDs) in total. Ideal for long car trips or for children to listen on their own. All seven of the *Narnia Chronicles* are included.

G.T. and the Halo Express
G.T. and the Halo Express is a useful tool for building Scripture memory by encouraging children to sing along. Children can repeat along with G.T.

Sir Bernard the Good Knight
In *Sir Bernard the Good Knight,* children can listen to lively music learning about friendship and adventure and twelve chivalric virtues: friendliness, obedience, thrift, courtesy, trustworthiness, kindness, helpfulness, cheerfulness, bravery, loyalty, cleanliness, and reverence. The character of Sir Bernard is based off of Bernard of Clairvaux, an eleventh-century, God-fearing monk.

Adventures in Odyssey
Adventures in Odyssey is the classic Focus on the Family children's production that teaches values and faith through adventure and lovable characters.

Aslan Academy Gatherings
Creating a Community of Parents Focused on Discipling Their Children

Parents have the responsibility and joy to disciple their children, but having a community around them can certainly help them as they go on this exciting journey. **Aslan Academy Gatherings** are designed to build a community of parents within the church who will commit to being intentional about discipling their children.

Getting Started

For parents, what can be more important than discipling your children to grow into mature, effective believers for Christ? Unfortunately, too many parents expect the Sunday school teacher or the youth pastor to fulfill this role. If a child spends two hours a week in church activities, that represents roughly .01 percent of the child's time for the year, not nearly enough to shape a child effectively. We believe that parents, working together to share ideas and pray for one another and their children, can make a huge difference in the lives of families and the life of the church.

The **Aslan Academy Gatherings**, which could occur monthly, can be a place to share ideas, exchange resources, pray for their families, and be encouraged. The **Aslan Academy Gatherings** can be organized by the children's director at a church or by a proactive parent who seeks to assist others in this common goal of discipling their children.

So you'd like to host a gathering, now what? Below are some ideas to help get your **Aslan Academy Gatherings** started. Each group can and will look slightly different from the other, as they'll be shaped by the individuals and families in the group. Perhaps your youth director or children's director would be willing to offer additional guidance. Most pastors would be thrilled to know that parents are interested in taking a proactive role in discipling their children.

A Recommended Agenda for Aslan Academy Gatherings

- Invite other parents in your child's Sunday school class, youth group, or neighborhood, clearly describing the purpose of the gathering.

- Meet at your church or in someone's home.

- Open with prayer, specifically asking the Holy Spirit to teach the parents and guide the children to spiritual maturity.

- At a first gathering, have parents introduce themselves and share about their families. It is important for everyone to feel comfortable knowing each other and sharing a desire to more effectively disciple their children.

- Share your successes and struggles. To begin, choose one of the resources from the *Aslan Academy* website and offer the key teachings from it and describe how that teaching may have helped you.

- Provide a Biblical foundation for the Aslan approach using the Bible studies in the *Aslan Academy* curriculum.

- Once the meetings begin, identify a book (or portion of a book) for parents to read in advance of a meeting. Then facilitate a discussion of that book at the meeting. Depending on the book, the group might use two meetings to discuss a book.

- Ask for a volunteer to prepare, for the next meeting, a five- to ten-minute presentation about an *Aslan Academy* resource he or she has used (other than the assigned reading), for example, an insight learned from reading a book or an experience in using a Bible storybook or other resource with their children.

- Encourage each parent to sign up for the *Aslan Academy* free monthly newsletter, the *Dawn Treader News*, which will provide ongoing encouragement, practical guidance, and helpful resources.

- The children's director or a lead parent can offer a challenge or suggest a specific project that parents can tackle in the coming month, perhaps drawn from the suggestions in the *Dawn Treader News*.

- Have one person take notes each meeting regarding helpful tips that are shared. If you desire, please share these with the group and with us at aslanacademy@cslewisinstitute.org so that we might share them with other groups. Other groups will be encouraged and inspired by your group!

- End with prayer and encouragement.

Notes to Leaders of Aslan Academy Gatherings

Introduction

There are two primary areas of responsibility for **Aslan Academy Gathering** leaders:

(1) Organizing an **Aslan Academy Gathering**, including selecting the initial resources to read and recruiting parents to participate.

(2) Serving as the leader/facilitator of a small group (generally consisting of no more than twelve parents).

An **Aslan Academy Gathering** will often consist of a single small group. A parent establishing such a gathering may serve both leadership roles.

Alternatively, a church children's director or other church leader might organize a larger **Aslan Academy Gathering** where the participants are divided into several small groups, each with its own leader/facilitator.

These notes address both leadership roles, which may or may not be filled by the same person.

Why Lead an Aslan Academy Gathering?

Would you like to be part of a community of parents within the church who are committed to being intentional about discipling their children? To see other parents become more effective in helping their children to know and trust Christ?

Or, if you are a church children's director, would you like to help parents form such a community within your church?

If your answer is yes, we at the C.S. Lewis Institute encourage you to organize/lead a small group for an **Aslan Academy Gathering**.

We believe you will be thrilled at the results that take place in your life, the lives of your children, and the lives of others. The dynamics will only partially depend on the thoughtful reading, Bible studies, and group discussion offered through the program. The growth will come through the power of the Holy Spirit as He works in the hearts of those going through the program.

This program could be used in a home group or perhaps as a larger gathering meeting at a church in the evening.

Choosing an initial book(s) for an Aslan Academy Gathering

We recommend that parents read and discuss selected books as a key part of **Aslan Academy Gatherings**. This will provide a focus for group discussion and content that will help parents grow in their ability to effectively disciple their children.

To let prospective group members know what an **Aslan Academy Gathering** will be about, the leader should select and announce at least the first book that will be read; the leader may want to announce the first two or three books.

We recommend that the books be selected from the resources in the *Aslan Academy* Guidebook. A number of the recommended books include discussion questions; these books are identified in that section by an asterisk.

Once an **Aslan Academy Gathering** is underway, the group may wish to discuss together what books to read next.

Other resources that might be used in Aslan Academy Gatherings

The **Aslan Academy Guidebook** includes several Bible studies and short articles for parental preparation, for example, "God's Plan for Parents"; "Reviewing the Fundamentals"; "Heart Change"; "Developing Character and Faith That Lasts"; and others. An **Aslan Academy Gathering** could use one or more of these as the basis for group discussion at a gathering, perhaps instead of a book for a particular meeting.

The **Aslan Academy Gathering** leader might also ask parents to volunteer to share about a particular *Aslan Academy* resource that they have read or used with their children. For example, a parent might offer a ten-minute "book report" on an *Aslan Academy* resource they have read—some insight they received or how they applied what they learned with their child.

Assigned Readings

The **Aslan Academy Gathering** leader should advise members in advance of what books or other resources to read for upcoming meetings. Depending on the group members and particular book, we generally suggest that a book be discussed over two meetings. In such a situation, the assigned reading for the meeting would be either the first half or second half of the book.

How many months should an Aslan Academy Gathering last?

We suggest that the leaders of an **Aslan Academy Gathering** commit to holding the gathering for a set period of time, with a view toward prayerfully considering what next steps to take as the end of that period approaches. For example, a person organizing an **Aslan Academy Gathering** might announce plans to host a once-a-month meeting between September and May, that is, a period corresponding to one school year. As the end of that time approaches, members of the group could discuss whether they would like to continue that gathering and, if so, who would lead/host, whether to break for summer or have other kinds of summer get-togethers, whether some of them might wish to host new gatherings, and so forth. If members of an **Aslan Academy Gathering** find that it is helping them and their children grow spiritually, they may wish to continue the gathering for many years.

The role and responsibilities of an Aslan Academy Gathering leader:

1. Pray

Throughout the process of planning and leading an **Aslan Academy Gathering**, it is essential that leaders pray for God's leading and direction. Pray that God would use you for His purposes in planning/leading an **Aslan Academy Gathering**, and pray that He would bring the right people to the gathering. Pray regularly for each parent who is part of a gathering, and for each family and each child. Pray that all parents would grow spiritually as a result of the gathering and grow in their ability to effectively disciple their children to know and trust Jesus Christ.

2. P-L-A-N

Before you begin the planning process, prepare for the process by reading this leadership guide and other *Aslan Academy* materials. Then begin the steps of planning:

Purpose. Know the purpose of an **Aslan Academy Gathering**: that you and your fellow parents learn how to more effectively disciple your children so they can know and trust Jesus Christ. Determine how you can best communicate the purpose of this program to the people you intend to invite to participate.

Logistics. Determine the logistics of:

When: When will you meet (date, time, for how long)?
Where: Where will you meet (home, church)?
What: What will you need to do to prepare the place for the meetings (seating, lighting, room temperature, beverages, snacks, childcare, removal of distractions, etc.)?
Who: Who will take care of the various planning pieces? Don't be afraid to delegate. People like to contribute and actually become more committed when they play a role in the group, even if it's just preparing refreshments or setting up chairs.

Some possible roles include:

Leader
Assistant Leader
Hospitality Coordinator
Childcare Coordinator
Facilities Coordinator

Activities. The **Aslan Academy Gathering** program has suggested activity plans for different types of groups. If your group has time to meet for a meal or even dessert, the fellowship over food can help build relationships and thus enhance the overall experience.

An **Aslan Academy Gathering** could meet on a once-a-month or twice-a-month basis. What would be best will depend on the context, e.g., the needs and overall schedules of the participants, whether the Gathering will be a home group or part of a program organized by a church, etc. Similarly, the length of each session (e.g., 90 minutes, 120 minutes) may vary depending on the same considerations, as well as on whether a meal is included.

Leaders may want to vary the amount of reading for participants to complete in preparation for each meeting depending on how often the group meets and on the length of each meeting.

Below are a couple of suggested formats.

90- to 120-minute sessions are ideal.

Sample *Aslan Academy* Gathering Agenda (Total: 90 Minutes)

10 minutes	Social time
5 minutes	Introduction of agenda for meeting and opening prayer
5–10 minutes	Short insight from Bible study related to the assigned reading
5–10 minutes	Summary Report by a parent on the assigned reading
25–35 minutes	Discuss assigned reading (using questions included in the relevant book, if available)
10 minutes	Sharing by a Parent about an *Aslan Academy* resource (other than the assigned reading), e.g.,
	• an insight gained from reading one of the recommended books
	• an experience using one of the Bible story books or other *Aslan Academy* resources with their children
10 minutes	Discussion of prayer requests
10 minutes	Closing prayer (including time for anyone who wants to pray)

Sample *Aslan Academy* Gathering Agenda (Total: 120 minutes)

40 minutes	Simple Dinner and Social Time (pizza, salad, drinks, and desserts—or a potluck)
5 minutes	Introduction of agenda for meeting and opening prayer
5–10 minutes	Short insight from Bible study related to the assigned reading
5-10 minutes	Summary report by a parent on the assigned reading
25–35 minutes	Discuss assigned reading (using questions included in the relevant book, if available)
10 minutes	Sharing by a parent about an *Aslan Academy* resource (other than the assigned reading), e.g.,
	• an insight gained from reading one of the recommended books
	• an experience using one of the Bible story books or other *Aslan Academy* resources with their children
10 minutes	Discussion of prayer requests
10 minutes	Closing prayer (including time for anyone who wants to pray)

Take some time well before each meeting to plan out the activities for the meeting so that things flow smoothly. Always start and end on time. People will get discouraged if the meetings go overtime or start late. If you desire, you can end the formal meeting on time and give people the option to stay later to fellowship or pray more. But always give people the opportunity to end at the prescheduled times.

Needs. Be on the alert to the needs of the people who are either in the group or may join the group. As you pray and ask the Holy Spirit to guide your planning process, He will give you guidance and help you determine the needs of your particular group and your responsibilities in meeting those needs.

Rick Howerton, in his book Destination Community, suggests some key questions to ask the Lord each week to prepare for small-group leadership:

Is there:
- Someone to pray with?
- Someone needing counsel?
- Someone to encourage?
- Someone to hold accountable?
- Something to celebrate with someone?
- Something to learn?
- A need to be met?
- A call to be made?
- A conflict to be resolved?

3. Prayerfully recruit participants

After planning, the second task of the leader is to prayerfully recruit the participants. Take some time to pray and ask the Lord to lead and point you to the right people to be in the group. Then begin inviting. Don't be disappointed if some say, "No, thank you." Persevere and keep on inviting until you get a committed **Aslan Academy Gathering** together.

Jim Collins, author of the modern leadership bestseller Good to Great, writes, "Great endeavors are accomplished best when the right people are in the right place doing the right thing." As you pray and ask the Lord to put together the right group, have faith that He can arrange the right people in the right place doing the right thing.

A personal invitation or a phone call is the preferred method of communication, as an impersonal e-mail might be overlooked and does not provide immediate conversational answers to questions. E-mail is great for follow-up.

Bobb Biehl gives the following advice in his book Mentoring:

"Don't hesitate—initiate."

You should be prepared to answer the following questions when recruiting people for the gathering. You might try to formulate an honest answer that you would like to hear if you were considering joining a group.

Be prepared to answer the following questions when recruiting a potential group member:

1. How much time will it take for me to prepare for and do the assigned reading/study for a meeting?

2. How long will the **Aslan Academy Gathering** last?

3. What kind of homework is involved?

4. Does it cost anything?

5. Do you have to know a lot of Bible or be able to pray out loud to be in the group?

6. How many people will be in the group?

7. What are we going to do in the meetings?

8. Who else is coming?

9. Do you provide childcare?

10. Would it be a problem for me to leave the group after a month or two if I find it's just not for me?

Group size: An **Aslan Academy Gathering** could be a single small group or a larger gathering with a number of small groups. It is recommended that discussion groups be small. It is hard to have interactive discussions with groups larger than thirteen including the discussion facilitator.

---

4. Develop a group covenant

Covenants provide a means of providing purpose, balance, and accountability within small group relationships. If people have knowingly signed a covenant, they are more likely to follow through on their commitment. What's more, the covenant makes it easier for people to give grace and/or lovingly confront someone who is not living up to the covenant.

For example, if someone is regularly missing the group's meetings, the leader of the group can say, "Hey, we've missed you recently. Your contribution is important and necessary for our group to function and grow. What can we do to help you make it to the group next meeting and fulfill your covenant?"

One of the first things a group can do to assure success is to agree upon a covenant. A covenant needs to take into consideration both the principles and logistics needed to achieve the group's goal. It would be wise to write up your covenant and then distribute copies to everyone in the group. Have the group discuss it and express any concerns or reservations about it. It can be adapted to meet the needs of the group as long as it doesn't compromise the mission of the program.

Some of the key components might include:

Attendance: a commitment to attend the meetings for a set period of time barring an unexpected emergency.

Preparation: a commitment to do the homework and to come prepared to the meetings. However, if participants haven't finished the homework, they should be encouraged to come anyway so that they can benefit from the group's discussion and get back on track.

Prayer: a commitment to pray for the group and that the Holy Spirit would help everyone grow spiritually through the program.

Confidentiality: anything shared in the group must stay in the group and not be shared with others. This is an important part of the covenant as it builds trust when maintained and allows people to be more open.

Openness: a willingness to share and participate in the discussions.

Honesty: a commitment to being honest and forthright in all relationships within the group.

Sensitivity: a commitment to being sensitive to the needs of others in the group.

Love: a commitment to love those in the group as commanded by Christ Himself.

5. Facilitate discussion

The great thing about an **Aslan Academy Gathering** is that you don't have to be a theologian or biblical scholar to lead a gathering. All you need is to be a committed follower of Jesus Christ who wants to be part of a community of parents who are intentionally teaching and equipping their children to become effective disciples of Jesus. Having said that, you will be asked to facilitate the group discussion.

The *Aslan Academy* identifies excellent resources that will help prepare parents to effectively shepherd their children to become committed followers of Jesus. Many of these resources include discussion questions. You can use these questions in leading a discussion, adapt them, or use questions of your own to get people talking. The key is to get others talking rather than doing the talking yourself.

An "ask, don't tell" policy is a good approach when leading the thematic discussion. Usually people should be ready to talk after completing the assigned reading in preparation for the gathering.

Some things to remember:

- Remember the questions who? what? when? where? why? and how?

- Give people time to answer. Don't answer your own question. Rephrase it if you'd like, but don't be afraid of "pregnant pauses." Someone might be ready to birth an amazing response, but it takes time sometimes.

- Be affirming by using expressions such as "Great insight"; "You're on the right track; can you expand on that?"

- Repeat responses as a way to get people to continue talking.

- Don't ask yes/no questions. If you do, have people expand their answers.

- Redirect people if they start to get off track. It's alright to politely interrupt and ask them to get back to the question or the main idea of the conversation.

- Don't go off on rabbit trails—lingering topics outside of the focus of the meeting.

- Don't let one person dominate the conversation. Politely ask to hear from others in the group.

---

6. Start and end on time
This point was stated earlier but is crucial to maintaining the morale of your group. If you meet the expectations of your group when it comes to the beginning and ending time of your meeting, you'll be trusted with other things later on. Be trustworthy in the little things, such as timing, and people will begin to trust you on more important matters. People live busy lives and need to know that they'll be dismissed on time. If you go late, you may lose people in future meetings. Also start on time, cluing people to the importance of arriving on time. If people know you'll be starting late, they will begin arriving late; it's just human nature.

7. Model what it takes to grow from the gathering by preparing yourself for the group discussion
In other words, practice what you preach and complete the assigned reading and preparation for leading the group before the gathering.

8. Use the *Aslan Academy* resources
If you find that you have a question about leading an **Aslan Academy Gathering** to which an answer can't be found in the materials, feel free to contact the C.S. Lewis Institute. The website of CSLI is www.cslewisinstitute.org.

9. Pray and enjoy the gathering!
Pray for the members of your group and pray that the Holy Spirit would guide the discussion. Pray that all distractions would be removed during the meeting. Do the work, show up to the group, facilitate the discussion, get to know the people in your group, and enjoy the gathering!

10. Follow up
Send an e-mail after the meeting, perhaps mentioning a highlight or two from the meeting and remind the group of the next meeting date/time.

2014 C.S. Lewis Institute©
8001 Braddock Road, Suite 301 • Springfield, VA 22151
703/914-5602
www.cslewisinstitute.org

C.S. Lewis Institute

Discipleship of Heart and Mind

In the legacy of C.S. Lewis,
the Institute endeavors to develop disciples who can
articulate, defend, and live faith in Christ
through personal and public life.

Get the *Aslan Academy* monthly update, the *Dawn Treader News*, at the C.S. Lewis Institute website www.cslewisinstitute.org/aslanacademy.

Made in the USA
Lexington, KY
30 November 2016